D1492387

On Foot in the Cairngorms

On Foot in the Cairngorms

V. A. FIRSOFF

Illustrated by the author with photographs, maps and line drawings

W. & R. CHAMBERS LTD.

Edinburgh and London.

Some Other Works by the Author

Scottish
THE CAIRNGORMS ON FOOT AND SKI
ON SKI IN THE CAIRNGORMS
ARRAN WITH CAMERA AND SKETCHBOOK
IN THE HILLS OF BREADALBANE

Scientific
LIFE BEYOND THE EARTH
EXPLORING THE PLANETS
STRANGE WORLD OF THE MOON
SURFACE OF THE MOON
THE MOON (in *The Age of Science* series)
MOON ATLAS
OUR NEIGHBOUR WORLDS
THE CRUST OF THE EARTH (in *The Young Scientist* series)

General
SKI TRACK ON THE BATTLEFIELD
THE TATRA MOUNTAINS
THE UNITY OF EUROPE

© *V. A. Firsoff, 1965*

Printed in Great Britain by McCorquodale & Co. Ltd., Glasgow, Scotland

CONTENTS

LIST OF ILLUSTRATIONS

THE CAIRNGORM MOUNTAIN

1 Ben Macdhui (4,296 feet).
2 Braeriach (4,248 feet).
3 Cairn Gorm (4,048 feet).
4 The Lairig Ghru Pass (2,733 feet).
5 Cairn Lochan (3,983 feet).
6 Sgóran Dubh Mór (3,635 feet).
7 Creag an Leth-choin, or the Lurcher's Crag
      (3,448 feet).
8 The Fiacaill Ridge
9 Bynack (3,574 feet).
10 Srón na Lairig (3,860 feet).
11 Coire an t-Sneachda, or the Snowy Corrie.
12 Coire an Lochain.
13 Coire Beanaidh.
14 Coire Ruadh.
15 Coire an Lochain (of Braeriach).
16 Cárn Eilrig (2,435 feet).
17 Creag Dubh (2,781 feet).
18 Geal-chárn (3,019 feet).

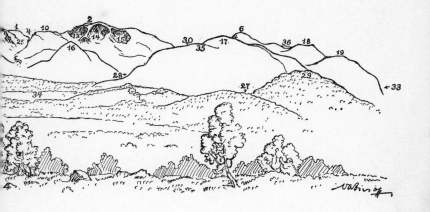

19   Creag Mhigeachaidh (2,429 feet).
20   Creag a' Chalamain (2,579 feet).
21   Airgiod-meall (2,118 feet).
22   Creag Chaisteal (1,465 feet).
23   (2,305 feet) ⎫
24   (2,237 feet) ⎬ Craiggowrie.
25   The March Burn.
26   Indicates the position of Loch Morlich in
       Glen More.
27   Indicates the position of Loch an Eilein.
28   Gleann Einich.
29   Ord Ban (1,405 feet).
30   Indicates the position of Loch Einich.
31   Coire Cas.
32   Indicates the position of Loch Pityoulish.
33   Glen Feshie.
34   The Rothiemurchus Forest.
35   Cadha Mór (2,324 feet).
36   Cárn Bán Mór (3,443 feet).

Rocks shaded. Heights and spelling after the O.S. Map.
The outline is drawn with a slight vertical exaggeration, to facilitate identification.

ACKNOWLEDGEMENTS

It is a pleasant duty to acknowledge the help received in the preparation of this volume in the form of advice and information in respect of:

The Invercauld Cairngorm from Captain A. A. C. Farquharson of Invercauld;

Jean's Hut and some minor particulars from Mr. Eric Langmuir, Principal of Glenmore Lodge;

The depths of the Cairngorm Lochs from King's College, Taunton, Somerset;

The Ordnance Survey in this and some other connections; and to thank Mr. Tom Weir for the use of his fine negative for the background view on the jacket.

Finally, I feel indebted to the Scottish Mountaineering Club and the Cairngorm Club for the use of some walking times and distances appearing in their publications.

INVERNESS

Spey

CAIRNGORMS

Dee

ABERDEEN

PERTH

GLASGOW

EDINBURGH

CHAPTER ONE

The Cairngorms on the Map

Now that the Space Age is upon us it seems meet to view the Earth from some orbital craft—rocket-propelled or, if you are Adamski-minded, a flying saucer poised high above the atmosphere. For my part I can claim no more of having thus viewed the British Isles than in some photographs taken by the *Tiros* weather satellite, but I have no reason to dissent from the Russian lady astronaut who has found them very beautiful. Perhaps not quite the Shakespearean " precious stone set in the silver sea," but rather a fretwork of pastel shades, diluted with atmospheric blue and laid out upon the inky velvet of the ocean whereover fleecy clouds are strung in wind-patterned flocks . . . the paled greens and the reddened browns, with here and there the grey of cities beneath industrial haze.

Northwards the browns prevail, transfused in autumn with the purple of ling in bloom. Among it, too, there are greyish areas, the largest of which lies about the middle of the great eastern lobe of Scotland. Yet the air over it is clear. It shows some structure, but not of the orderly man-made type, is veined with green and brown, perhaps etched with a little white, and splashed and streaked with the ocean-dark of water. Obviously not another London! Should this area be close to the evening or morning terminator during our orbital over-flight it will be lined with deep shadows, gathering into semi-circular scoops near the edges. The long shadows may exaggerate the vertical relief, but any experienced astronaut, human or un-human, will recognize the area, even if unable to pin to it the name of Cairngorms, as mountains. He, she or it may also ponder on the comparatively wide acreage of high ground, from whose barrenness they derive their greyish hue.

Indeed, the Cairngorms are the largest compact mountain area of Britain, comprising 200 square miles above the 2,000-foot contour, while its summit plateaux exceed the 4,000-foot mark in five different localities and approach it in many more. The structure of the hills well remembers the recent Pleistocene Ice Age, and they have a climate to match.

North-westwards our area is bounded by a broad valley, studded with numerous lakes and dark-green with pinewoods, down which a river threads its way to Moray Firth. This is Strathspey. The valley carries the trunk road and rail route that spans nearly the length of Britain and so forms a natural approach to the Cairngorms. In the west the narrower glen of the Feshie, which falls into the Spey near Loch Insh, cuts off the high Cairngorms from the lowlier browner hills beyond, and its line is continued by the Geldie Burn, which trickles eastwards over desolate moors to the Dee. The Dee rises right in the heart of the mountains and so opens up a natural gateway into them. Once more pinewoods crowd darkly, though less massively than on Speyside, into the glens, and a rail and road follow the river from the east, the latter up to the Geldie itself and a little doubtfully beyond. Another road branches off south at Braemar over Glen Clunie and Glen Shee to Perth and the populous Lowlands.

A further thin cobweb of non-arterial macadam creeps along the lesser rivers of the north and crosses here and there the heathery uplands. But directly south, between Strathspey and Glen Shee, the land is almost as roadless as it was when General Wade first tackled the problem of Highland communications from the military viewpoint after the Jacobite rising of 1715.

The Dee makes a reasonably clear boundary of the Cairngorms from the White Bridge and the Geldie to an arbitrary point where

Gleann an t-Slugain runs out on to it at Invercauld. Our space observer would probably make the course of the Quoich Water and the Gairn a natural march of the Cairngorms, but the people down below have decided otherwise and traced it along the rough road from Invercauld House to Bealach Dearg (Red Pass) and only thence along the Gairn as far as Loch Builg.

Loch Builg and the Glen of that ilk delimit the Cairngorm area naturally enough up to Inchrory and the Avon in the north. The course of the Avon is the northern march as far up as Ath nam Fionn, the Fingalians' Ford, at the foot of A'Choinneach and Beinn Mheadhoin, whence the march skirts the slopes of the high peaks, crosses the Nethy and completes the circuit at the Pass of Ryvoan. Westwards of the latter the Kincardine Hills thrust out towards the Spey and are usually reckoned part of the Cairngorms, with some geological misgivings.

As much our visitor from space could not divine, but he could make out the division of the Cairngorms into three segments: the Western, Central and Eastern by the deep passes of the Lairig Ghru and the Lairig an Lui. A map is not unlike a space view, but it shows the district with more human circumstance, if less physical directness.

A space view is not very suitable for judging even such aspects as the quality of roads, and one certainly could not guess from it that the Cairngorms lie at the meeting point of three shires: Inverness, Banff and Aberdeen, that they contain a vast National Nature Reserve and a Forest Park, nor, of course, any of the placenames.

There are various maps of the district in existence, but many of them are obsolete in such vital respects as roads, bridges, chair-lifts and mountain shelters. The three sectional maps of the mountains included in this book are as up to date as possible, but owing to their small scale do not cover the whole of the area, and their possibilities are also limited by the use of only one colour (black on white). The most comprehensive, newest and undoubtedly best from a hill-walker's point of view is the One-

Inch Tourist Map of the Cairngorms, issued by the Ordnance Survey in 1964. It shows not only the mountains themselves, with most of the latest amenities, but also the approaches from Spittal of Glenshee in the south to Grantown-on-Spey in the north, and from Kincraig in the west to a point 3 miles short of Ballater in the east.

The physical information conveyed in a map is not exhaustive. Rocks are shown, and steepness can be inferred from the crowding of contours and to some extent from the course of the streams, which tend to run straight over steep ground and meander over boggy flattish areas. Yet, in practice, a descent over screes from Cairn Toul to Lochan Uaine or to Coire nan Clach from Beinn a'Bhùird presents no serious difficulty, despite the fearsome aspect of the map, while, contrariwise, the thin fringe of rock indicated in Coire Bhrochain of Braeriach conceals some of the most imposing mural precipices in the whole of the Cairngorms. Gentle ground at the foot of a steep slope may be expected to be wet, but this is not shown in any of the maps, nor are tiresome boulder-screes and awkward long heather. Long heather will not usually grow on ridges and shoulders exposed to the wind, but may be found on lower slopes in the shelter of high peaks or corries. Boulder-screes are the product of rock decay and so are to be expected on steep mountain sidings in association with crags, past or present, where the decay is most rapid, for instance on the western slopes of Braeriach, which are exposed to the prevailing wet winds.

Such simple rules are useful in interpreting a map and planning a tour or climb without other information. There exists a further rule of the thumb which may be a help: fair touring progress in average weather may be reckoned at 3 miles per hour, adding a further half-hour for every ascent of 1,000 feet.

A map is a vital necessity, but it is of small value without a compass with which to orient it by reference to recognizable landmarks. The quarters of the sky as given in my maps and most other maps refer to the National Grid system, which does not deviate much from the true north, but the difference between

Loch Morlich.

May in the Lairig Ghru.

the Grid North and the Magnetic North as shown by the compass is at present about 9½ degrees, the latter being this much west of the Grid North, and neglecting the correction may lead to trouble.

Strathspey is the most accessible as well as the most populous part of the Cairngorm piedmont. Its towns and villages have direct train connections, not only with Edinburgh and Glasgow, but with London, and are within an overnight journey of most British cities. Kingussie, Kincraig, Aviemore, Boat of Garten, Nethybridge, Carrbridge, and Grantown-on-Spey are the main centres of Speyside and stations on the railroad, which branches at Aviemore and again at Nethybridge. Kincraig and Aviemore with Coylumbridge are undoubtedly best placed for exploring the Cairngorms without private transport.

In the east Inverey, known as the climbing headquarters of the Cairngorm Club, based on Aberdeen, and the new tourist establishment at Mar Lodge are very well located as a base for the Central and Eastern Cairngorms alike. But the main centre of population on upper Deeside is Braemar, three miles farther down the river and 17 miles from Ballater, which is the railhead on the line to Aberdeen. The small village of Crathie, in the shadow of Balmoral, lies halfway between the two. Except for the village of Tomintoul, eight miles by road (dubious) north of Inchrory, there are no other noteworthy settlements elsewhere within an easy reach of the Cairngorms.

All those listed, however, have hotel, boarding-house and hostel accommodation to offer, as well as houses for summer letting, though booking well in advance is to be recommended, as the demand is brisk. Sometimes it may be possible to obtain rooms or sleeping quarters in the cottages at the foot of the hills, but these possibilities are very limited and not to be counted on at the height of the season.

Owing to the recent development of forestry and ski-ing, Glenmore has now become quite a settlement. It contains a youth hostel, and the Scottish Council of Physical Recreation runs an outdoor training school at Glenmore Lodge, an ultra-

B*

modern building in Scandinavian style, with courses in hill walking, rock climbing, pony trekking, ski-ing, etc. It does not, however, offer accommodation to casual visitors, for whose convenience the Forestry Commission has provided a camping ground on the alluvial flat at the head of Loch Morlich. Glenmore is linked by a driving road with Coire (Corrie) Cas, where a chair-lift operates summer and winter between a car park at about 2,100 feet above sea-level and a point some 500 feet below the summit of Cairn Gorm (4,084 feet), thus giving ready access to it and the mountain land beyond. Refreshments can be obtained at the White Lady Shieling in Coire Cas.

The Rothiemurchus Hut at the western entrance to the Lairig Ghru is not open to civilians, but only to members of the three Services (without distinction of rank or sex) upon appropriate application. It can accommodate about 40 people. The use of Derry Lodge, which has been leased to the Cairngorm Club, is similarly limited to members of this club and affiliated clubs.

The map will show several bothies, which can be used in emergency, but are often in ruinous condition. These have been erected primarily for deer stalkers and game keepers, but Corrour Bothy and the two Memorial Huts, in the Lairig Ghru and Coire Etchachan, are of solid construction and intended to be used by walkers, climbers and skiers without club or other restrictions. A part of Faindouran Lodge in Glen Avon is also open to visitors without charge. It must, however, be borne in mind that the Cairngorms are uninhabited over most of their area, such huts, bothies and shelters as there may be are few and far between, and they consist for the most part of bare walls and roof, with at most a fireplace and bunks, so that food and bedding must be carried by anyone intending to stay there. Crossing the mountains is a matter of some 20 miles of rough walking, which may be very strenuous in bad weather and should not be undertaken without due care, experience and physical fitness.

Some crossings, such as the Lairig Ghru, with a clear path, are straightforward enough; others are not. Much of the

Cairngorms can be most confusing in bad visibility. There are extensive stretches of featureless plateau or moor with hardly any clear landmarks to aid orientation, and losing one's way may lead to aimless wandering and exhaustion that has been known to be fatal.

Two emergency refuges in the form of concrete cells embedded in cairns have been provided on the eastern slopes of Cairn Gorm, but they are not too easy to find, despite the pole with a bell that tolls in the wind with which one of them (St. Valéry Refuge above Coire Raibert) has been provided. The Shelter Stone at the head of Loch Avon may also be reckoned as a refuge. Elsewhere there is nothing at all.

It is not my object to frighten people off the Cairngorms, but to inspire some respect for these mountains in those who do not know them or have not seen them in their angry moods.

CHAPTER TWO

Blue or Red?

THE Cairngorms take their name from their northernmost four-thousander Cairn Gorm. As seen from Grantown-on-Spey and farther north, where the greatest neighbouring concentration of population is to be found, Cairn Gorm stands out on the horizon as a handsome shouldered cone, beyond which the rest of the mountains spreads in a summitless plateau. This is how *A'Chàrn Guirm*, to give the mountain its correct Gaelic name, has come to be the titular chief of the clan, an office in which it has now been confirmed by the recent development of Glen More as a tourist and ski-ing centre.

As befits a language of mountain-dwellers, the Gaelic has a wealth of words to describe mountain shapes. *Beinn*, which has passed into Scots as ' ben,' is a mountain in general; *càrn* or *a'chàrn* with the article, becoming ' cairn ' in Scots, is a heap-like pointed one, best rendered in lowland English as ' peak '; *meall* (myall) or *maol* (mell) denotes a rounded hill; *monadh* (' dh ' is silent) conveys a gentle outline; so does *mullach* (' ch ' as in loch), which though is extended like a roof; *sgùrr*, *sgòr* or *sgòran* is the Norse *skur*, *skaur* or *skuran*—a sharp, cutting summit; *fiacaill*, used for ridges between corries, is a misappropriation of the Scandinavian *fjall* or *fjäll*, meaning simply mountain; and, finally but not exhaustively, *creag* (craig) is the English ' crag ' or Scots ' craig ', which are both derived from it.

On the other hand, while there are two words for red: *ruadh* (rooah) and *dearg* (jerg), and at least three for grey: *glas*, *liath* (' th ' silent) and *odhar* (our), blue and green are oddly confused in a single one—*guirm* (goorm) or *gorm*, although pale green is *uaine* (pr. as *ouagne* would be in French).

Thus the Cairngorms are ' Blue Peaks,' a not very fitting appellation, which is clearly due to people who did not know them very well and perhaps ' had ' little Gaelic.

Any mountains seen from the distance are blue, and so the Cairngorms appear from Moray or Nairn, but this is by no means peculiar to them. Their true character is revealed far more truthfully and impressively at closer quarters, from Aviemore and thereabouts (*see* the panorama on p. viii.). Their summits are flat, and their majesty—for they have that!—lies in the rocky corries gouged in their sides. Bedight in autumn tints, they stand apocalyptically stark—an arctic vision of Stone Age hills in plum and russet soaring over the Caledonian Forest, or what remains of it.

Indeed, the Gaelic-speaking locals were far more discerning and called the Cairngorms *Monadh Ruadh*, the Gentle Red Hills, after their reddish granite screes, in contradistinction to the grey schists of the *Monadh Liath*, the Grey Mountains, on the other side of the Spey.

Nor is, of course, Cairn Gorm their highest peak. This distinction belongs to Ben Macdhui, second only to Ben Nevis in the mountain hierarchy of Britain.

The latter rises in the company of the Aonachs above Fort William at the westernmost end of the Grampians, where its huge bulk looms unrivalled over the sea. Yet, after all, there is not such a lot of difference between Ben Nevis's 4,406 feet and the 4,300 feet of Ben Macdhui. And Ben Macdhui, whether it take its name from an hypothetical MacDuff or a black hog (*muic dubh*), which the mountain is said to resemble to a Gaelic eye, can count in its close vicinity on three supporters exceeding 4,000 feet: Braeriach (4,248 feet), Cairn Toul (4,241 feet) and Cairn Gorm (4,084 feet). This in the days of clan feuds gave the squatty Ben a decided ascendancy over his rival at Fort William. For Ben Macdhui had been thought to be the loftiest summit of the country until, in 1810, Dr. Keith's barometer dissented from public opinion in giving Ben Nevis a stature higher by fifty feet.

Regional pride was deeply stung, and the adherents of Ben Macdhui would not give in for a long time, while any mention of that Ben at Fort William was fraught with personal danger. Yet 37 years later the sappers, who " paid handsomely," as the local story goes, and were responsible for the erection of the huge cairn embedding a minor obelisk on Ben Macdhui, made a detailed survey of the Grampians and degraded the peak to its present position. John Hill Burton is said to have been ready to go down on his knees and implore the surveyors to reverse their verdict, but to no avail. The dispute continued to rankle, and a project was seriously entertained of ' adorning ' the summit of Ben Macdhui with a ' sepulchral vault ' of such size as to outtop Ben Nevis.

Today this is past history, but I am not too sure that all the flames of the old controversy have been finally quenched. Anyway, writing in 1925, the Rev. John Stirton does not go beyond the somewhat cautious statement that Aberdeenshire includes " *Ben Macdhui*, said to be the second highest mountain in Great Britain " (*Crathie and Braemar, A History of the United Parish*, p. 7; Aberdeen, 1925). You never know but the surveyors may, after all, have made a mistake!

So here we are with Ben Macdhui, the three other four-thousanders, and Beinn a'Bhuird (3,924 feet) and Ben Avon (3,843 feet) as the ' Six Cairngorms,' which have all been ' done ' in one day—no mean feat, even though aided by the lie of the land whereby the ' Six ' stand in pairs linked by high ground, so that little climbing is required between them.

As we already know (p. 3), the Cairngorms are split into three distinct segments by the ' passes ' of the Lairig Ghru and Lairig an Lui. The term ' pass ' in this case means not so much a depression between two peaks as a crossing or ' mounth ' leading from the one to the other side of the mountains. The Lairig

Ghru is a nearly straight cut across the body of the Cairngorms, from Aviemore to Braemar, 27 miles apart. It takes in the upper Glen Dee, but may still be described as a conventional ' pass.' The Lairig an Lui (Laoigh), on the other hand, is not a coherent unit at all. Leading from Abernethy to Braemar, the mounth first follows the Nethy, then threads its way over the lower slopes of the Bynacks to Lochan a'Bhainne and its nameless col, whence it runs down along Allt Dearg to Ath nam Fionn, crosses the Avon to Dubh Lochan and the pass between Beinn Mheadhoin (3,883 feet) and Beinn a'Chaoruinn (3,553 feet) to Glen Derry, which it descends to Glen Lui and Glen Dee. It is the concatenation of all these features and not the col, for which the Gaelic has another word, *bealach*, between the two bens, that makes the *lairig* (pr. larig).

The Lairig an Lui is much the longer of the two, but was supposed to be easier. In any event the drovers used to take mature cattle to and from the Aberdeenshire markets over the Lairig Ghru, but thought its boulder-screes too rough for the tender feet of calves, which were driven over the Lairig an Lui instead. Indeed, Lairig an Lui means the Calves' Mounth. The etymology of *Ghru* is doubtful, but it may be an abbreviation of *grumach*=gloomy, which seems fitting enough. The two lairigs were also the established routes of seasonal labour in broad daylight and of " infamous bykes of lawless lymmars " (chiefly cattle reivers, but not averse to violence) on some more misty occasions, and of warring clans.

Thus in 1527 the Grants of Rothiemurchus raided the Deeside Shaws over the Lairig Ghru, wreaking great slaughter and leaving a multitude of orphans, who were afterwards brought by the Earl of Huntly to his castle and fed there like swine from a trough. Half of them were subsequently adopted, kindly, by the Clan Grant and nicknamed, unkindly, " The Race of the Trough." The affair was the subject of some ' compositions ' embodied in ' notarial instruments,' but more than this was needed before the last of it had been heard.

During the Civil War Montrose marched his army over the

pass, having taken the wise precaution of dumping his cannon in a bog on the way up.

On another occasion, which was a Hogmanay, three jolly tailors, having, no doubt, consumed more whisky than a good mountaineer should, died in a snow-storm beside a boulder, known since as Clach nan Taillear (the Tailors' Stone), on their way over the Lairig Ghru. Today the walkers are protected against such mishaps by the existence of two shelters on the two sides of the pass.

On the Aviemore side the Angus Sinclair Memorial Hut, containing iron beds and cooking facilities, stands about 1½ miles below the highest point where the walking path crosses the Druie Burn (Allt Druidh) and is joined by the track that leads to Glen More over the gap of Creag a'Chalamain. Corrour Bothy, first built in 1877 and completely refurbished in 1950, is a more substantial construction at the foot of the Devil's Point four miles down the Dee, which has one of its springs in the Pools of Dee in the Pass of the Lairig Ghru, a quarter of a mile south of its highest point. Corrour Bothy is away from the path across the young river, over which an iron footbridge was erected in 1960.

Wading the river could be dangerous in spate, as it still is at Ath nam Fionn where the Lairig an Lui track crosses the Avon. According to an old saying, " the water o' A'an (Avon) rins sae clear t'wad beguile a man o' a hunner year." Men of a hundred years are clearly not to be encouraged to ford the Avon there, but I found it awkward, too, and traditionally the Lady of Fingal was swept there off her feet and drowned . . . ohone!

There are no huts in Lairig an Lui, except for Derry Lodge and the possible hospitality of Luibeg Cottage at the foot of Glen Derry, but the Hutchison Memorial Hut, comparable to the Angus Sinclair one, is about a mile off the track up Coire Etchachan on the way to Ben Macdhui and could be sought out for shelter in unweather.

Be it as it may , the two lairigs split the Cairngorms into three segments, between which the Six Cairngorms are partitioned equally two by two.

Ben Macdhui and Cairn Gorm belong to the Central Cairngorms, as do the Bynacks, More and Beg, Beinn Mheadhoin (pr. Bein Main or Vain), Derry Cairngorm (3,788 feet) on the other side of Coire Etchachan, Càrn a'Mhaim (Carn a Vam 3,329 feet) above the Lairig Ghru south of Ben Macdhui, and Cairn Lochan (3,983 feet) and Creag an Leth-choin or the Lurcher's Crag (3,448 feet), which rises in a rocky triangle over the Aviemore part of the Lairig Ghru defile, in the north.

Braeriach (4,248 feet), Cairn Toul (4,241 feet), The Angel's Peak or Sgòr an Lochain Uaine (3,950 feet), The Devil's Point (Bod an Deamhain, 3,303 feet), Sgòr Gaoith (3,658 feet) and Sgòran Dubh Mòr (3,635 feet), known jointly as ' The Sgorans,' Càrn Bàn Mòr (3,443 feet), Meall Dubhag (3,268 feet), Monadh Mòr (3,651 feet) and Beinn Bhrotain (3,795 feet) are the main high tops of the western division.

The Eastern Cairngorms comprise Beinn a'Bhùird, having a North Top of 3,924 feet a.s.l. and a South Top of 3,860 feet about two miles apart, Ben Avon, which is a complex of summits, attaining 3,843 feet in the tors of Leabaidh an Daimh Buidhe (Lebay an Dow Booie=Couch of the Yellow Stag), Cnap a'Chléirich (pr. Crap a Leyrikh=Clergyman's Knoll, 3,811 feet), and Beinn a'Chaoruinn (3,553 feet) and Beinn Bhreac (Ben Vriac, 3,051 feet) as independent Munros over the Lairig an Lui.

Nearly all of the Western Cairngorms and part of the Central fall within the Cairngorms National Nature Reserve, while the Speyside slopes and corries of the Lurcher's Crag, Cairn Lochan, Cairn Gorm and its subsidiary heights to the Pass of Ryvoan, as well as most of the Kincardine Hills, lie within the Glen More Forest Park. All this land is open to the public, who, however, are not allowed to remove plants, bring in heavy machinery, dogs, horses or other animals without a special permit. The making of fires and—in the wooded areas—smoking are likewise prohibited. The object is to preserve the character of the area intact, but without restricting the normal agricultural use of the land, including forestry, to which the Forest Park is particularly dedicated.

The building of chair-lifts, ski-tows and roads leading to these has not, however, been deemed inconsistent with the aims of the Glen More Forest Park, nor did the Nature Conservancy object to the building of the Sinclair Memorial Hut, which is just within its boundaries, and to the reconstruction of Corrour Bothy.

CHAPTER THREE

Scenery and Geology

GEOLOGY was born in the mountains. Nowhere else are the workings of its forces and processes imprinted so clearly on the landscape. Once geology is called in, order emerges from the apparent chaos and many land features become predictable, making mountains easier to understand and live with.

The primary rocks of the Earth's crust are of two types: the dark and heavy basic rocks, and the lighter and brighter acid rocks, which naturally overlie them according to gravity, much as oil floats on water. The basic rocks are found chiefly in deep-ocean beds, but they also occur in a few land localities where they have been poured out in molten condition on to the surface as basaltic lavas, say, in the Plateau of Antrim, or intruded under the overlying strata and become exposed as gabbro after these strata have been removed by erosion, as in the Black Cuillin of Skye.

In the Cairngorms there are no basic rocks at all, but they are still important, down below, twenty or more miles underground, where they are hot and plastic like pitch upon which the land is buoyed as though on an elastic rubber cushion.

All primary rocks are igneous. They have crystallized out of the molten mineral mixture, called magma, sometimes slowly, in which case the component crystals are large, sometimes quickly, yielding small crystals, and very occasionally, when appearing on the surface as lava, they have had no time to

15

crystallize before setting and appear as undifferentiated volcanic glass. There is none such to be found in the Cairngorms, for, unlike many western districts of Scotland, these mountains are not volcanic.

The rocks of the Cairngorms are all acid and of the most common kind, composed of felspar, quartz (silica) and mica. When slow-cooled and coarsely crystalline such rock is called granite. When the rock has cooled rapidly in small intruded masses the crystals are so small that they cannot be easily distinguished with the naked eye and it becomes felsite. An intermediate condition of cooling results in large crystals scattered through a micro-crystalline matrix. This is porphyry. All the three kinds occur in the Cairngorms, and since there are no sharp boundaries between the different conditions of cooling, any intermediate texture is possible.

Most of the Cairngorms granite is coarsely crystalline and weathers readily to sharp grit, but more resistant portions of finer grain are likewise present, while in the veins or dykes of pegmatite, or giant granite, the individual crystals may be measured in inches.

So primary rocks are igneous, but when exposed to air and water they are subject to weathering and erosion. Expansion and contraction due to heat and cold, especially in the presence of moisture, the chemical action of carbon dioxide and oxygen from the air, the mechanical force of the wind, running water and sliding ice, slowly but steadily wear down even the highest and hardest rocks to rubble, grit, sand, clay, mud and silt, which are carried away by streams and winds, to be deposited on low ground, mainly in the sea. Thus the surface of the land is being levelled down to a plain, while sediments continue to build up till they grow miles thick, are compressed and sink deeper and deeper under their own weight. Compression and heat from within the Earth turn them to hard secondary rocks.

Such ancient, highly compressed and partly recrystallized sediments are usually finely layered, like streaky bacon, and called schists. As the process continues they eventually return to the original composition of granite. The wheel has turned full circle.

There is, however, a stage where sandy sediments are very nearly but not quite granite yet. This is granulite.

Granulites and schists are the peripheral rocks of the granitic Cairngorms. They are of immense but uncertain pre-Cambrian age, which may be a 1,000 million years or more. These rocks contain no fossils, which makes them difficult to date. It used to be thought that there was no life on Earth at the time of their deposition, but modern study has moved the origin of life further and further back.

All that life had been given at the beginning was granite, water, air—a pretty nasty kind of air with a lot of methane and ammonia and no oxygen—and the energy of sunlight. Yet it has managed and, after 3,000 million years of evolution, has produced the chair-lift on Cairn Gorm and the Beatles . . . Think of it as you kick a granulite pebble by the Youth Hostel in Glen More.

The Cairngorms are nothing as ancient as all that. Barely some 350 million years ago, in the Silurian, was the part of the Earth's crust that is now Scotland and Scandinavia convulsed by great folding movements, which gradually upraised those granulites, schists and still later sediments, a part of which is exposed as limestone in Glen Builg, into the mighty Caledonian ranges. As the strata were pushed up into folds, acid magma poured into their roots from the bowels of the Earth, to set into hard granite batholiths, which is the Greek for ' depthstone.'

This was the beginning of the Cairngorms.

In their prime the Caledonian Mountains rivalled the Himalayas. Water streamed and avalanches roared down their faces, glaciers crept along their valleys. The forests of giant horsetails and club-mosses had come and gone, the poles and the equator had shifted their positions, the dinosaurs had reached the peak of their power and vanished, leaving the Earth to little mammals, including the tree-shrew—the ancestor of *Homo Sapiens*, and in the meantime the proud ridges had been worn down flat to their granite roots.

As, however, all this mass of rock had been removed, the resilient ' rubber cushion ' of the sub-crustal plastic basalt redressed itself. It was as though Mother Earth, freed from the burden, drew a deep breath and puffed out her chest, lifting the stump of the Caledonian Mountains into a high plateau. The elevation of the land quickened the flow of the streams, which bit deeper into their rocky beds and split the tableland into segments.

Thus the Cairngorms were born.

In the Tertiary, the Age of Mammals, Britain was a tropical land. There were palms and crocodiles in the Thames Valley. But, as the 70 million years of that age were drawing to a close, it grew colder and colder, until in the Pleistocene—a bare million years ago—huge sheets of ice crossed the North Sea, to join the glaciers forming on the British hills. In the end even the Cairngorms were buried beneath a thick carapace of ice, as the mountains of Central Greenland are today.

There were comings and goings, with interglacials when the ice disappeared and the climate was warmer than now, but each time the Arctic came back, the ice-sheets grinding down the upstanding rocks and widening the valleys.

This is how the High Tops have acquired their smooth, licked-up look, with rounded knolls and clean, polished slabs. The final (if it was that) retreat of the glaciers took place between 5 and 10 thousand years ago. By then the ice-sheets had gone and only the local glaciers remained, and it is these that have left the strongest mark on the landscape. Indeed, without the work of the ice, although a little more pointed here and there, the Cairngorms would have been a dull place.

The High Tops and the core of the mountains are coarse-grained granite with red felspar. This rock has wide-spaced rect-angular joints, which give the mural precipices of the corries an appearance of ' Cyclopean masonry.' It weathers to square-hewn scree, and the final product of its erosive degradation is the beautiful pink sand of the beaches of Loch Morlich, Loch Avon and Loch Einich. But the envelope of schist and other sedimentary rocks is preserved in the foothills, and the whole of the Kincardine Hills is, apart from some pegmatite dykes of pre-Caledonian age, granulite and schist, with flaky screes and hummocky outcrops.

These are the materials on which the ice worked, but at the height of glaciation ice flowed freely over the land, bringing in rock debris from other districts. These were spread wide and thick as *glacial drift* over Strathspey, bulldozed into a broad flat-bottomed valley by the piedmont glaciers. The thickness of the drift, with its ice-rolled boulders stuck in the clay like currants in a cake, can be clearly seen in the banks of Allt Mòr in Glen More or those of Allt Druidh at the entrance to the Lairig Ghru.

The distribution of the drift is uneven. It forms small hillocks, known to geologists as kames or drumlins and to the locals as ' fairy knowes,' and depressions that go by the name of kettle-holes. Wherever sufficiently deep and dammed by moraines, the kettle-holes are filled with water and become lochs. Loch Morlich, Loch an Eilein, Loch Pityoulish and most other lochs of Speyside are in this class. The kettle-hole lakes are not very deep as Highland lochs go, and the 300-acre Loch Morlich does not exceed 40 feet in depth.

Still shallower are the small peaty *dubhlochans*, so called from the Gaelic *dubh lochan*=black tarn, which are scattered in profusion over the lower moorlands and forests.

Glacial drift is highly suited for the growth of trees; and, as the glaciers and the arctic flora retreated to the High Tops, Scots fir and some scrub oak moved in on the heels of birch orchards until the green sea of the Caledonian Forest lapped high up the glens. During the so-called Climatic Optimum, about 4,000 B.C., the tree-line exceeded the 2,000-foot contour. Nearly the whole of the Lairig Ghru was thickly wooded, and I have come across remains of trees above the col between Càrn a'Mhaim and Ben Macdhui, nearly 3,000 feet up. Lower down the pines survived long enough to give the name of the Glen of Pines—Glen Geusachan (pr. Yoosahan)—to the now-treeless valley between the Devil's Point and Beinn Bhrotain.

Today the forest seldom oversteps the 1,500-foot line. This is due only in part to the deterioration of the climate, especially in the Roman times when it was wet and cold and the flourishing peat-mosses stifled young trees. Another cause must be sought in the renewed elevation of the land, which may have exceeded 100 feet to judge by some raised beaches, after it had been freed from the great weight of overlying ice. Thus, the old contours need not have coincided with the present.

Running water channels the ground into gradual V-shaped valleys, as can be seen in the ravines of the post-glacial streams, which have not had time greatly to affect the hills. Water, however, had been at work on the Cairngorms for millions of years before the Ice Age, and had wrought the V-shaped pre-glacial valleys to receive the ice. In a few cases water erosion had proceeded far enough to isolate cragless conical peaks, such as Càrn Eilrig above Rothiemurchus, or whet the land between two valleys into a long ridge, of which Càrn a'Mhaim is the one clear example in the Cairngorms.

Water chisels fine and narrow, but a glacier, moving on a broad front, works like a channel tool. It tears off and carries away obstacles on its sides, so that a glacier valley is of U-shaped cross-section, flat-bottomed with almost vertical sides. The superimposition of glacier erosion on pre-existent water forms results in an oversteepening of the lower slopes and the production of triangular rock faces where mountain shoulders and side ridges have been shorn away (Creag Mhigeachaidh, the Lurcher's Crag).

The level of the ice in the Cairngorm glens varied at different stages of glaciation and depending on the local conditions, but at the most persistent stage the local glaciers attained what is now the 3,000-3,250-foot contour, above which the glacial U does not extend. Here the ground breaks suddenly, often into a rocky scarp, the effect being particularly striking above Loch

Ben Macdhui, 4,300 ft., the highest Cairngorm.

Braeriach, looking down the precipice of Coire Bhrochain over the Black Pinnacle.

Avon. Thus in descending an unknown or unrecognized slope in the fog one can expect trouble at this contour, and conversely, when climbing, the easing-off of the gradients is an indication that the 3,000-foot mark has been passed.

The valley glaciers were fed by the eternal snowfields of the dismembered tableland. The amount of snow available for the glacier depended on the catchment area and the outlets from it. Round the edges the snow, compacted to ice, began to flow into the glen wherever it found a natural opening. On entering the glen it was compressed to a great thickness, which—we have just seen—may have exceeded 2,000 feet. This huge mass of ice exerted enormous pressure on the sides and particularly on the bottom of the glen, especially where the feeding grounds were high and wide and the outlets few, as happened on Ben Macdhui and on Braeriach with the adjacent plateau of the Great Moss.

Thus the Macdhui glaciers have gouged the rocky defiles of Loch Avon and Coire Etchachan, while those descending from Braeriach and the Great Moss have cut the wide gap of Gleann Einich and the boxlike recess of Glen Geusachan. The Lairig Ghru is of an earlier vintage and had been forced by the land-ice coming in from the east.

The entrance to Glen Avon and Gleann Einich was by way of a steep corrie, so that the incoming ice struck the floor of the glen at a high angle. The resulting pressure was sufficient over thousands and tens of thousands of years to remove great thicknesses of rock and to dredge in it a deep trough. The pressure decreased down the glen, so that the trough was deepest at the head and shallowest at the foot until it flattened out as the glacier was thinned by melting. At a later stage it did not extend very far down the valley and deposited at its foot the rock debris it carried in a mound of the terminal moraine. The size of the moraine varied depending on how long the glacier halted at this particular point, but a time would come when the retreating glacier dropped its terminal moraine so as to dam the rock trough it had worn out in earlier days, and as the ice finally

C

Loch Avon and Loch Etchachan

melted it was replaced by a long and deep valley-lake. Thus Loch Avon and Loch Einich have come to be.

These lochs were surveyed in 1953 by a party from King's College, Taunton, Somerset, and found to attain a depth of 115 and 160 feet respectively. At one time they may have been even deeper. Eventually, the silt brought by the streams and the screes dipping into the loch will fill up the basin and only a green flat will mark its site, but this will take some time. Except at the foot, the ground shelves down very steeply into the loch, making it dangerous for bathing.

Moraine tarns, or—to give them a homelier name—'corrie lochans,' resemble the valley-lakes in some respects, but are of a roundish outline, not so deep, and have a somewhat different origin.

A corrie glacier will not generally have enough mass to excavate a deep basin. Nor are the cliffs enclosing a typical corrie the direct effect of glacier erosion. They are due primarily to frost shattering.

Water seeps into rock joints and crevices and, since it expands in freezing, it splits the rocks open and so breaks them up into loose boulders. This mechanism will operate anywhere, and in the absence of a persistent snow-field—not necessarily a glacier —it will eat into the crags and simply reduce them to rough scree, as has happened in the western corries of Braeriach.

On the slopes, however, which face east and north or are otherwise sheltered from the sun and thawing winds, the snows of winter may become packed to a great depth and persist for many months even now. The snow will stay at or below freezing point regardless of the air temperature, but the dark rocks at its edges will be warmed by the sun and at contact with them the snow will melt during the day. In fact, summer snows are often bordered at the head by a deep gap, known under the German name of *Bergschrund*, due to melting at contact with the rocks. By night the rocks will be chilled by the snow to below freezing point and the melt-waters which have seeped into them during the day will freeze, giving rise to strong shattering action. Thus the snowfield will eat into the body of the mountain and under-cut the rocks, which will tend to overhang it. Eventually the overhang will peel off and the resulting debris, instead of accumulating at the foot of the rocks, will slide out over the snow to the foot of the field and pile up there in a growing mound.

If this process continues for long enough it is easy to see how vertical cliffs enclosing a moraine-dammed hollow are produced, making a natural setting for a corrie lochan.

The difference between a corrie and a glen is only one of degree, and in some cases glacier erosion may intervene as well more or less effectively to dredge a rock basin, so that a lake intermediate in character between a moraine tarn and a valley-lake will result. Loch Etchachan is a case in point. Yet this is not necessary, and corries and their lochans may arise without true glacier action.

When the snow precipitation was heavier cliff-rimmed corries may have formed just as readily on the western and southern sidings of the Cairngorms. Indeed, if the temperature of the air stayed low this situation could have favoured frost shattering. Few, however, of such western and southern corries have survived unimpaired to this day, while, though on a much reduced scale, the corrie-forming processes still operate during the spring months in many northerly and easterly corries.

From this it follows that if you lose your bearings in the clouds on the High Tops the safest course to steer is south-west.

This story explains the scenery of the Cairngorms: their wide flat tops, their precipitous corries, their lochs, the slopes of their high glens, steep below and gentle above, and the scarcity of sharp points or narrow ridges. The latter are almost wholly limited to *fiacaills* at the meeting of corrie cauldrons, and only one of them, the Fiacaill a'Chòire an t'Sneachda, is a true rock arete. Even so it is of moderate climbing difficulty, while the similar ridge of the Angel's Peak, although craggy, is of none.

CHAPTER FOUR

'Pellucid Stones'

THE 1795 *Statistical Account of Scotland* mentions "pellucid stones, of the nature of precious stones, equally transparent, beautiful in their colour, and some of them, particularly the emerald, as hard as any oriental jem of the same kind," found in the Cairngorms.

It is perhaps not too surprising that a Scottish stone should be "as hard as any oriental jem of the same kind," for hardness characterizes the mineral species, quite regardless of the colour and clearness of the specimen on which its 'gem quality' depends. But this does not affect the rest of the statement.

The layman is accustomed to associate definite colours with particular gemstones. The ruby is carmine or 'pigeon-blood,' the amethyst violet, the topaz yellow, the emerald green, the garnet red, and so on. He or she may be reconciled to the fact that ruby and sapphire are one and the same mineral, corundum (a crystalline form of alumina), and differ only in colour. But it comes as a shock to learn that sapphire may also be green, violet, yellow and even colourless—'like diamond,' which, too, can be of almost any colour.

There are green garnets and purple beryls. 'Scotch topaz' is a yellow variety of quartz, otherwise known as cairngorm, of which more anon. This is doubly confusing, as the real topaz, sometimes even expectedly yellow, is also found in Scotland, though the Cairngorm topaz is usually sky-blue.

To put it straight—in so far as possible—some colours are as it were indissolubly linked with the basic chemistry of the mineral. Thus the green variety of garnet known as uvarovite is never other than green. Most gem minerals, however, are colourless when chemically pure, and assume different colorations as a result of minor impurities. Several colours may even be present simultaneously in one and the same crystal.

Quartz can be colourless, yellow, of various shades of brown to nearly red and nearly black, pink, violet or bottle-green, but is still quartz, whatever the trade name given to the dressed stones. Its hardness is 7 on Moh's Scale, and it crystallizes in six-sided prisms with transverse striations. It also breaks with conchoidal fracture. This is how it can be recognized, though there are further tests, such as specific gravity and refractive index, to identify it.

Ideally the hexagonal quartz crystal is even-sided and terminates in pyramidal points at both ends. Such crystals *occasionally* occur in nature, but as a rule the different facets are unevenly developed, or several crystals coalesce in a single stone, which results in very complicated structures nothing like the theoretical. For such pitfalls you must be prepared if you go crystal hunting in the Cairngorms.

Quartz is a very common mineral and one of the three main constituents of granite. In an ordinary granite block, however, mica, felspar and quartz are chaotically jumbled; their crystals are small, intergrown and imperfectly developed, the quartz being usually milky-white. In this condition quartz is no gem. What makes a crystal worth the lapidary's work, apart from its innate hardness, is clarity, ' fire ' (i.e. a high refractive index) and colour.

Not only quartz; felspar, too, occurs in transparent crystals, and moonstone is a gem variety of felspar, which to the best of my knowledge is not found in the Cairngorms. But quartz crystals *are*, sometimes, of considerable size, both colourless, when they are referred to as rock crystal and fancifully as

' Occidental diamond '! (Pliny's ' diamond ' was, in fact, rock crystal) and in several colours.

Rock crystal is the lowest grade of gem and not much used in jewellery, although it can be quite attractive. Most quartz crystals found in the Cairngorms, however, are tinted with the oxides of iron and manganese. Iron alone yields yellow or brown stones, known as citrines and cairngorms respectively, and black morions. Typically a cairngorm varies from whisky through sherry to ginger, but the crystals from Ben Macdhui are reddish. The presence of manganese oxide may further modify the tint, in the extreme case producing wine-red stones that are sometimes classed as amethysts, though an amethyst proper is quartz coloured violet by manganese oxide without iron.

Amethysts likewise occur in the Cairngorms, but are nothing like as common as cairngorms.

In the second half of the nineteenth century, referred to as the ' Balmoral period,' a brooch with a large cairngorm became an obligatory part of Highland dress, though cairngorms have been used in the Highlands as occasional ornaments for many centuries before that. As a result the search for cairngorms became an important source of additional income to ghillies and gamekeepers, some of whom, on Seton Gordon's authority, died in this quest through drinking " water from gravelly burns."

Regular mining operations were instituted and deep trenches dug in crystal-bearing grit on Ben Avon and Cairn Gorm.

Some finds were quite spectacular.

One John Grant of Ryvoan found, in the bed of Am Féith Buidhe, the stream that descends to Loch Avon from Lochan Buidhe about halfway between Cairn Lochan and Ben Macdhui, a magnificent cairngorm, which weighed 50 pounds and which he presented to Queen Victoria. He was rewarded with the like number of pounds sterling, which was good money in those days.

Another highly successful crystal-seeker from an earlier age was an old woman nicknamed *Cailleach nan Clach* (Old Woman of the Stones). One night she dreamt of a splendid crystal beckoning to her from the rocks of Beinn a'Bhùird. She lost no time in setting out to find it, which—be it precognition, clairvoyance or mere luck—she did.

This was the famous Invercauld Cairngorm, believed to be the largest crystal ever found in Scotland. It weighs 52 lbs. and is some 2 feet long. The date of the find is uncertain, but the first mention of this stone occurs in a book by John Stoddard, published in 1799, so that *Cailleach nan Clach* must have dreamt her dream sometime in the second half of the eighteenth century. The stone is the property of the Farquhar-sons of Invercauld, and is now on show at Braemar Castle, which is open to the public.

The import of cheap foreign stones eventually killed the local cairngorm 'industry,' and nowadays the stones in 'Celtic brooches,' even when genuine and not 'paste' imitations, usually hail from Brazil, Germany or Madagascar. Still, some people like having a real Scottish stone, which is even better fun if you have found it yourself.

The Provosts of Blairgowrie wanted a chain of office set with Scottish cairngorms. These were not readily available, and nearly all of them came from my collection, except for a few purchased at Inverness, to make up the number.

Yet there are 150 square miles or more of granite in the Cairngorms, and its supply of crystals cannot have been exhausted, despite the 'mining operations.'

One often hears of 'blue' and 'green' cairngorms, which is a contradiction in terms, for *cairngorm* is brown quartz, and quartz found in the Cairngorm Mountains is never blue or green (bottle-green 'smoky quartz' occurs in the Alps). What is meant is topaz and beryl respectively.

The main components of granite are felspar, quartz and mica, but various other minerals may be associated with them in small amounts, especially in mineralized veins, where very hot magma, rich in gases, has entered fractures in consolidated rock, giving it a 'maggoty' appearance.

Tourmaline, garnet, topaz and beryl are among the most usual 'associate minerals' of granite, though some granites contain diamond, sapphire and spinel, as well as various metals. There is a little gold in all granites, and some silver appears to occur in the Cairngorms, to judge by such names as Argiod Meall—the Silver Hill.

Be this as it may, at least topaz and beryl are not uncommon.

Cairngorms topaz is usually of a pale-blue colour, in fact, rather too pale to make a good gem, but what it may lack in colour is made up for in size. Topaz 'boulders' a foot long have been found.

The mineral is a fluoro-silicate of aluminium of hardness 8 and crystallizes in four-sided orthogonal prisms with a roof-like summit. Unlike the horizontally striated quartz, topaz crystals are lined vertically, which together with the colour makes them easy to distinguish.

Beryl and Cairngorm

Beryl is hexagonal like quartz, but its prisms are usually much more regular, with vertical striations like topaz. In hardness it is half-way between quartz and topaz ($7\frac{1}{2}$ on Moh's Scale), so that it will lightly scratch the former and be similarly scratched by the latter. Owing to the tendency to split at right angles to the major (long) axis of the crystal, a beryl often has the shape of a flat-topped column, but it may also run up into a sharp point, grooved lengthwise on the sides, or else the flat summit may be bordered by small oblique facets. Chemically, the mineral is a composite silicate of beryllium and aluminium.

Pure beryl is colourless, but it assumes various colours depending on admixtures. In many specimens from the Cairngorms the colours are arranged in layers, starting with yellow and passing through green and blue into purple at the tip.

Yellow beryl goes by the name of ' golden beryl '; blue and green-blue (the commonest) varieties are aquamarines; purple beryl is called morganite. All these, as well as the leek-green beryls, topaz and coloured quartz, rank as semi-precious. But a beryl tinted a shamrock-green with oxide of chromium is true emerald, one of the most precious stones. A fine emerald may exceed diamond in price, although good emerald crystals can now be grown artificially, which has lowered the market value of this gem.

So, with luck, if you keep your eyes skinned in the right direction you may chance on this " oriental jem."

Yes, but where ?

The answer is that I do not know, and if I did I would not tell you. You should, however, equip yourself with a geological hammer, one or two stone-mason's chisels and some small digging tool. If you then follow the rules outlined below you should be able to find something—perhaps not an emerald, but at least a cairngorm.

Good crystals seldom develop in compact rock. But hot magma contains gases in occlusion which are liberated in the cooling and form bubbles in the hardening rock. The walls of such bubbles, which are called druses, are usually lined with crystals of the component minerals of granite. The size of the crystals is, of course, related to the size of the druse. Drusy rocks may occur anywhere, but very often cavities develop where the rock has been intruded while still semi-plastic by additional sheets and veins of hot magma, carrying a lot of gas. If the rock looks ' maggoty ' it is a hopeful sign.

Grain size depends on the rate of cooling, and large crystals will not grow in rapidly-cooling magma, so that fine-grained granite seldom has much to offer. But if you come upon a vein or dyke of giant granite (pegmatite) of extra-large grain and it contains druses (rounded cavities) or vuggs (long chained cavities) you may expect some real ' whoppers.'

It is, however, no easy matter to extract a crystal intact from live rock. I have encountered some hollows lined with splendid cairngorms, big as fists, but quite ' ungetatable.' Therefore, the old-time cairngorm-hunters—those *cailleachan* (old women) and *bodachan* (old men) *nan clach* (of the stones)—used to trace a promising rock formation to where it entered a scree-shoot or grit and dig there. Well-formed, sound crystals do not readily succumb to weathering and may in such conditions be found loose in the grit, which saves a lot of trouble.

But don't drink water from ' gravelly burns '! Rather take a leaf from J. G. Francis's *Beach Rambles in Search of Seaside Pebbles and Crystals*, published in 1861, where a crystal-seeker is advised to " carry a flask of any liquid he likes best to imbibe; together with a hunch of bread and cheese. . . . Lastly, a few mild cigars, not omitting the usual implements for striking a light *sub divo*." In other words,

> " Oft taste the cordial drop,
> And rest, O rest, long,
> Long upon the top!"

CHAPTER FIVE

The March of Seasons

How much truth is there in the old weather saws and signs? I once considered this question in *Scottish Field* (February 1962), partly independently and partly on the basis of earlier investigations, with the conclusion that much of the traditional weather lore is based on sound observation, but with a generous element of superstition and purely fanciful analogy.

The effect of the different winds is thus summed up in an old Gaelic saying:

> " South wind, heat and produce;
> West wind, fish and milk;
> North wind, cold and tempest;
> East wind, drought and withering."

The climate of the Cairngorms differs in some respects from that of the rest of the Highlands, but mainly in the great exposure to the wind of their high unsheltered plateaux, and in relative dryness due to the inland situation, away from the Western seas. Indeed, the annual rainfall average for the Cairngorms is only 30 inches, as compared with say, 100 inches at Fort William. Yet, with some local variation, the general effect of the winds is much the same as elsewhere, and it does not agree too well with the quadric.

Thus, a south wind can be cold in spring and winter, and quite wet in autumn, even though a south-east one is usually hot and dry in summer and one of the snow winds of winter. Nor does a north wind bring cold and tempest; quite the contrary, it is a good wind, usually associated with fine weather, if perhaps rather icy nights. North-westerly winds mark the passing of an atmospheric low; they are squally, with thundery outbreaks and sunny periods. The stricture applies properly to the north-east wind alone. The Gael does not seem to have been too particular about the points of his compass—perhaps he had none.

Officially the year begins at Hogmanay, just as the week does on Sunday, but neither fits the realities of life. Sunday is the ' weekend ' and Monday starts off the activities of the next seven days. Similarly, the natural renewal of the annual cycle of life does not come in January, but with the first stirrings of spring.

Occasionally a Cairngorm spring does come in a big rush, with the birches dressed in new-minted green gold, the larks singing and the curlews piping over the moors. But more often than not it seeps in imperceptibly. It grows warmer and warmer step by step. Blizzards alternate with spells of hot sunshine. A flower opens here, a green leaf appears there, as the winter retreats to the High Tops, the gullies and corries still gleaming white when it is already summer in the glens.

The first intimation of change comes in the midst of frost and snow. Grey cloud, edged with foxy russet, overspreads the sky. The air grows mild and muggy, yet somehow heady. The snow sags and loses its lustre. It will be drizzling, or the wind from the west will roll billows of cloud over the hills.

There is a touch of sombre fullness in the view. The nearer hills are damson-dark, and now and then subdued dun lights blossom forth on their sides and fade away. Dense gloom has gathered into the corries. Mist whispers on the boulders and is blown into dim shapes escaping over the snow. It seems as though at any moment strange animals may come down from the tops into the brown, snow-streaked glens, or a band of ghostly warriors pass by on a secret foray. The giant footfalls of the Grey Man of Ben Macdhui may still be dogging the lonely walker in the mist, and the Spectre of Glen More nursing his bleeding hand in search of someone to challenge to a deadly combat.

A few days will pass and winter will reassert itself in black and white, but the snows continue to recede, and by the end of March their cover is usually broken even on the High Tops, though substantial ' wraiths ' may persist in sheltered places into June, or longer. Should this be so a hill-walker or scrambler who has steep snow-slopes to negotiate is well advised to carry an ice-axe, for these summer snows are treacherous; a slip on the snow is difficult to check and may prove fatal. If, however, an ice-axe is gripped firmly by the head and either the pick or the adze end pressed into the snow one can stop sliding almost at once. Otherwise the spring months are very good for mountaineering of any grade, for the weather is often fine at this time of year, and the average precipitation is reduced to a third, the air is dry, there are no clegs and midges to contend with, and it is not too hot for climbing even with a heavy pack.

So, gradually, the pulse of life quickens. Dark spots and patches appear on the white winter coats of ptarmigan, blue hare and stoat. Birch twigs turn a deeper wine, and buds are turgid with suppressed growth. Tortoiseshell butterflies and Red Admirals emerge from their winter slumber, and perhaps even a Camberwell Beauty, an occasional immigrant from Scandinavia. Stray bumble-bees buzz over the snows in search of early flowers. Purple saxifrage, one of the relics of the Ice Age, flowers as early as March, but it does not grow on granite, where its place is taken between 2,500 and 3,500 feet, in the ' middle arctic zone,' by creeping azalea, which bears small wine-coloured blooms in late spring and sometimes again in autumn.

The drama of the Cairngorm climate is dominated by the trial of strength between the south-west and the north-east wind, the one a spirit of lax moist warmth, the other of stern crystalline cold. The westerly and south-westerly winds account for about 50 per cent of all winds in winter, but the proportion of the north-easterlies rises to 11 per cent in spring; while both follow the main lie:of the land with its valleys and ranges running south-west and north-east.

Other winds do not enjoy the same freedom of movement and are but passing visitors. The age-long feud is between the Nor'easter and the Sou'wester.

The two winds come early to grips with each other. It will blow persistently from the south-west in the opening months of winter, thawing up the snow brought by the north-easterly gales and sweeping it into the corries facing that quarter of the sky, until, seeing his work ruined, the Nor'easter is goaded into a rage. This will come as sure as day, and he will fling himself upon the hills, to spread his arctic dominion over top and glen, drive people, cattle and sheep into the shelter of roofs and walls, finally giving way to anticyclonic conditions, with pale veiled skies and ' inverted ' temperatures. It will then be warmer on the tops than down below, as the heavy night-chilled air flows down-slope and collects in the glens, bringing the temperature lower and lower. If anticyclonic conditions persist long enough the thermometer may drop as low as 50°F. of frost, as it did in 1944 and 1947, but this is exceptional. Anticyclonic systems are very steady, yet sooner or later a depression will move in to the north or north-west of the British Isles and give the Sou'-wester his chance.

In he will come, roaring, from the wide Atlantic Sea, to bring relief to man and beast, leaving the wintry hills streaming with water, and peat-brown burns trundling boulders in a fury of foam. This will be the Sou'wester's first attempt at spring, but it will not last.

Seeing his old enemy's triumph, the Nor'easter will be stirred to new efforts. It may be summer-warm in mid-March and early April, then a spell of bitter weather will recap the hills with snow, bringing business to the chair-lift and ski-tows. These are the so-called Lambing Storms, which will have blown themselves out by early May, when a warm sunny period is due, but if the usual writ runs the end of the month will be cold and heavy snows will revisit the Cairngorms.

This time they are not much use to anybody, not even to skiers, and the frost that often comes with them may spoil the crops, singe young leaves, and nip the promise of fruit and berry in the bud.

June is one of the dry months, though often far from flaming, with cool days and a good deal of cloud in the sky, and the early half of July continues the trend to fine weather. But, as the school holidays draw near and summer visitors begin to throng in, a grey canopy comes down upon the bens and cold mists spread over the pewter lochs, shivering with the gooseflesh of small ripples. The ' gods of the weather ' seem to take a dim view of the ' Glorious Twelfth,' when it usually pours cats and dogs. Indeed, the typical British August is one of the wettest months of the year, and the Cairngorms are no exception to the rule.

Yet there is beauty in a wet grey day, too, especially if it comes after a hot spell when the sun has lain scorching on the nape of your neck and overheated air danced over the rocks and raised dust devils on the road.

The thin ' Scotch mist ' descends like a transparent veil on to the hushed world. Green secretive dusk has gathered in the pinewoods in restful communion with Earth, the ageless goddess of whom all things fleet of limb and green of leaf take life. Pine stems are the rough columns of a pagan temple. Star-moss is soft and deep. The heavy dew has diluted the verdure of grass to a pale silken brightness. The hand of autumn has already touched the bracken with gold, and the ling is in full bloom. The eye can revel in its amethystine glow for mile after mile of hollow and brae till it fades out, pink in the distance, at the grey edge of the cloud.

Sketched lightly in faded water-colours, the hills are a glimpse of life's forfeited promise, within perpendicular gates of white mists slowly travelling by, the hills of a dream or the hills of a saga, their feet in the heather, their brows in the sky . . .

Be this as it may, August and the opening weeks of September are amongst the worst times for hill walking—wet and windy,

The Cairngorms from Craigellachie, Aviemore, with the corries of Braeriach outlined in spring snow.

Springtime at the edge of Loch an Eilein.

with midges and ' clegs ' abroad in their millions. But the close of September and early October are often marked by days of crystal calm and wide blue horizons. The nights are already chilly, and hoar-frost will silver the summits at dawn, to melt into glittering dew-drops in the morning. At noon it will often be hot, but never with the oppressive heat of summer, and the mountain shadows are already cool with the foretaste of winter. The reds, russets and yellows of autumn are set out against the dark lochs and blue distances in an unforgettable symphony of colour.

Indeed, late September and early October are excellent for the hills. The days are still long, and the ' gloaming ' evening skies provide several hours of pleasant twilight for the return trek. Most of the visitors have gone, and with them the difficulties of overcrowding. The only snag is that this is the rutting season of the red deer and the stalking season of those who come to shoot them at their nuptial feast. The stalkers do not like to have the herds disturbed by walkers, and bullets fly a long way and may be indiscriminate in the choice of accidental targets. Still, there is no law of trespass in Scotland, nobody can object if you follow the right-of-way paths, and stalking takes place in the glens and corries and not on the High Tops, even where the ' ancien régime' is still in force, as it is in the Eastern Cairngorms . . .

One day in the second half of October I awoke at Achlean, in Glen Feshie, on a pink morning, with thick silvery dew on the heather bidding fair for a walk on the High Tops. The stalking path took me to the summit of Càrn Bàn Mòr (3,443 feet) at the edge of the Great Moss, where creeping willows showed yellow in the matted growth.

Càrn Bàn Mòr by itself is not an exciting mountain, but it gives access to the Sgorans, which soar 2,000 feet in rocky ribs and steep scree-shoots above the dark mirror of Loch Einich, beyond which Braeriach bulges hugely, its boulder-screes livid against the acrid ochre of sedges and the copper of bracken. And the ridge of the Sgorans was my destination.

D*

Below the summit of Sgòr Gaoith two coveys of plover whirled up at my approach and 'peeled off' downslope, steering with their pointed wings. The English for Sgòr Gaoith would be Windy Point, and windy enough it is as a rule. This time, however, the air was hardly stirring by its summit cairn where I sat for two hours doing a pen sketch, lightly dressed, without the slightest discomfort in the warm sunshine.

When, at about four, I reached Geal-chàrn, following the declining ridge, the westering sun had spread above valley and hill a wake of silver dust, in which the streams and pools of water glittered like fragments of a gigantic mirror shattered by the angry hand of some forgotten goddess of the Druidic past. Mountain ranges paled away in the distance, blue shadows in a blue sky, until they were lost in it. Westwards the ash-grey moss shimmered like hoar-frost on the stones, and, tipped with the first dew of the evening, the scarlet blaeberry leaves shone like rubies, sown among it with a generous hand. From Allt Ruadh came a faint aroma of pine resin, mingled with the sharp scent of sun-heated herbs.

The ticking of my watch was the loudest sound. Then a fly buzzed, a stag's challenge rolled down from the Black Sgòran, and from somewhere aloft came the chirping of invisible small birds heading south on migration flight.

My way led down the steep ruins of rocks, grown over with mats of crowberry and golden-moss, from which white ptarmigan rose on whispering wings and glided in an oblique curve down into the cool shade of the lowly pass. The sun was a red ball of fire when I reached the edge of Creag Mhigeachaidh (Vigayhay). Loch Insh lay below, a dull silver tray among the curly blonde heads of the birches.

The scramble down the screes of the Creag through scraggy pine thickets was laborious and slow, and dusk was gathering quickly in the broad glen of the Feshie, where the golden ghosts of a birchwood closed round me, trying to confide to me some lisping tale of joy or sorrow, the key to whose meaning I had lost with childhood.

The road up the glen wound pale over the darkening moor, and the rabbits scampered off at my approach, their white scuts twinkling in the heather.

Soon after, the weather broke over the hills, though it remained fair over Strathspey. Persistent south-easterly winds, on being chilled by the ascent, blew along the High Tops a fleece of cloud which rushed in cataracts down the north faces of Braeriach and Cairn Gorm, dissolving in sleet and rain, and disappearing almost without a trace. I had to face a furious onslaught of the wind in the Lairig Ghru, and was drenched and numb with cold in a matter of minutes at the Pools of Dee. The icy blast forced me back from Sròn na Lairig, but it was dead-calm and the sun shone bright and hot a thousand feet lower down on the top of Càrn Eilrig, only two miles to the north-west. The northern corries of Braeriach were already grey with the first fall of snow.

Indeed, quite heavy snows are not unusual at the end of October, but they do not last. Christmas is normally ' black ', but the New Year comes white. A heavy fall of snow is often followed by a day or two of great calm and sunshine, and it is a Scottish mountaineering custom to ' first-foot ' the hills on the First of January. If the weather is fine and you are suitably dressed there is no reason why you should not do it, but it must be borne in mind that the day is short, so that the itinerary must be carefully planned and an early start is a necessity.

In general early winter is not a good time for visiting the High Tops, where the thermometer sinks very low and fierce winds spring up suddenly and range freely over the icy wastes. Combined with low visibility this situation can be suicidal to the inexperienced, and the experienced will mostly have the sense to stay away at such times. Yet no devil is as black, or in this case ' as white ', as he is painted, and I have known some beautiful days of sunshine and snow at this time of year in the High Cairngorms.

Their winter climate and its exigencies are considered in more detail in the companion volume, *On Ski in the Cairngorms*.

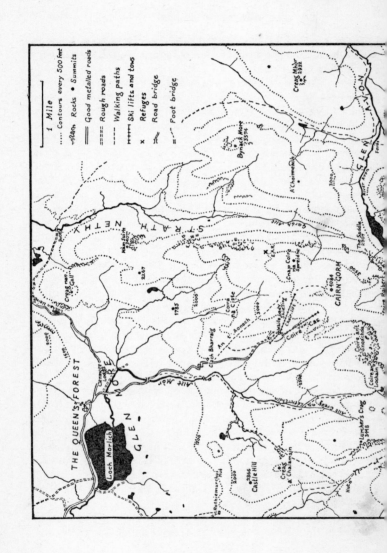

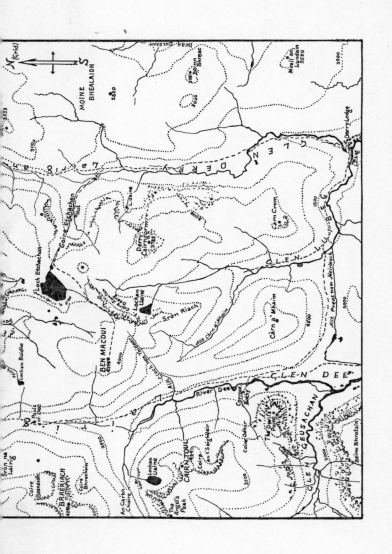

CHAPTER SIX

The Grey Heights

THE Central Cairngorms are contained, east and west, by the two Lairigs, which meet where the Lui Water falls into the Dee. Thus the central division of the mountains forms a deep wedge between the other two. It is the smallest of the three in area, but also the highest, and comprises some of the finest scenery the Cairngorms have to offer.

Here the high granite tableland has been whittled down by ice and water into a kind of discontinuous horseshoe, whose hollow part cradles the narrow waters of Loch Avon (pr. A'an). This is a true valley-lake (see p. 23), over 100 feet deep and, bar a northerly gale, calm within the shelter of its crags. Small sickles of pink sand nestle among the boulders at its lower, shallower end. Lying at 2,377 feet a.s.l., the loch is frozen for several months every winter; yet it holds char and trout, if no longer the beautiful but mischievous kelpie, said to have been captured by a wily man of Tomintoul who surreptitiously slipped a silver bridle over its head.

One-and-a-half miles long but only 450 yards at the widest point, the loch occupies the site of a pre-glacial valley, which is continued beyond the lowly Saddle (2,707 feet) by the line of Garbh Allt and Strath Nethy, but the ice from Ben Macdhui, probably impelled by a reinforcement from Cairngorm, swung east and broke a gap between Creag Dubh and A'Chòinneach. Down this the young Avon, fed by the clear waters of the loch, pursues its course to Inchrory. The Saddle and Glen Avon form the two natural approaches to the loch.

The glacial scarps on its two sides are less than a mile apart at the 3,250-foot contour, where the gentle pre-glacial slopes rise to what remains of the high tableland in the wide ridge of Cairn Gorm and the warted heights of Beinn Mheadhoin (Vain, 3,883 feet). Uphead the Shelter Stone Crag and Càrn Etchachan rise like towers of black granite up to 600 feet over the screes, and the white waters of Garbh Uisge (Rough Water) thunder down from the grey mass of Ben Macdhui to the green flat of the Dairymaid's Meadow and are hushed in the loch.

The summit plateau between Cairn Gorm and Ben Macdhui is from a mile to two miles wide. Its central backbone does not sink much below 3,900 feet, except at Lochan Buidhe (Yellow Tarn), which lies at 3,683 feet amidst a broad saddle, providing a natural crossing from the Lairig Ghru to Loch Avon, and drains impartially into both, by the March Burn and Am Féith Buidhe respectively. The rocks in the lower part of the latter can be by-passed on the right towards Garbh Uisge, while the course of the March Burn is steep, with some rock on the sides, but presents no serious difficulty.

Lochan Buidhe is shallow, but it is a permanent sheet of water and has a valid claim to be considered the highest mountain lake in Britain. On a hot day a dip in the lochan may be refreshing, but at most times it is decidedly uninviting, a bleak windswept place.

Northwards, after a gentle rise, the ground is nearly flat for about a mile, and its highest point, roughly halfway between Cairn Gorm and Ben Macdhui and 2½ miles from either, is marked with a cairn (3,983 feet), from which it takes the name of Cairn Lochan. The cairn is perched at the rim of a forbidding black precipice of ' Cyclopean masonry ', rather poorly ' mortared ', with a lot of loose stones and shaky holds to worry a climber making his way up from the corrie below. This is Coire an Lochain, and it duly contains a small tarn at its western end.

The cliffs can be evaded on the sides: in the west easily, and in the east more awkwardly, over steep scree and grass at the edge of the Fiacaill Ridge, which divides Coire an Lochain from the Snowy Corrie, or Coire an t'Sneachda in Gaelic (pr. Corrie an t'Rayakh if you please).

The Fiacaill is of scrambling difficulty with one or two easy climbing pitches which are safely negotiable without a rope to experienced mountaineers, but those to whom this description does not apply will do well to avoid it for the easier slopes below. In the east the ridge has a rock face abutting at the screes of the Snowy Corrie, which make at this point a quick descent route but may be awkward on the way up, as the gradients are steep and there is a lot of loose stuff shifting under your feet. Farther on, towards Cairn Gorm and the next fiacaill, the crags close their ranks and have no scrambling routes to offer. Under snow both corries are climbing propositions throughout, except for the westernmost end of Coire an Lochain, where the ground slopes gently towards Glen More.

On the other, south-eastern side of the ridge, Loch Avon is girdled with rocks of awkward disposition. But the girdle has been broken by the burns at two points, which provide natural ways up and down, to or from the loch. These are Coire Domhain (pr. Down), leading over boulder-screes, enlivened with parsley ferns and rich oases of mountain vegetation, straight to the Shelter Stone; and Coire Raibert, about a mile farther down the Lochside. The St. Valéry Refuge stands at the upper edge of the rocks halfway between the two corries (see map).

Coire Domhain is easy enough even in bad visibility, but in coming up Coire Raibert it is advisable to keep to the burn, not to lose the bearings. There is a lot of rock about, which may begin quite innocently as seen from below and then steepen up nastily in the fog, making retreat hazardous.

South of Lochain Buidhe the ground swells gently towards the summit cairn of Ben Macdhui, so gently in fact that when the view has been swallowed by cloud—the Grey Man apart—it is not always easy to tell whether one is going up or down and one place looks very much like another. Fortunately, there is no shortage of cairns marking the path.

There are no precipices in the west, where the sidings of the Lairig Ghru are harmless, if steep, at any point between Lochan Buidhe and the summit. In the east, however, scarps and ice-smoothed bluffs abound, and not all of them have handy by-passes, such as at the head of Loch Etchachan. So it is better to stick to the cairns.

The horseshoe as a whole dips north-eastwards, where the gate of Loch Avon gapes wide to the arctic gales that sweep down from the pole with a depression over the North Sea. When this happens the air temperature on the high tableland may fall below freezing even in summer, and in winter the mere task of survival becomes a problem enough. This is grey, barren country, where the refugee flora of the Ice Age can alone maintain itself in patches.

The hardy growth of least willow (*Salix herbacea*), furry with catkins in the autumn, carpets thickly the loose grit of the Cairn-Gorm-Cairn Lochan ridge, if this wide strip of ground deserves the name. Only the leaves show above the ground, but the willows are proper trees, with a tiny stem that may have taken decades to mature and branches concealed in the grit, which shields them from wind, drought and frost. Here and there a little sedge and grass has secured a foothold in a sheltered hollow or the lee of a rock. It is too high even for creeping azalea (*Loiseluria procumbens*) and crowberry (*Empetrum nigrum*), low woody growths which resemble each other in leaf, except that the latter bears shiny, watery black berries, rather like little buttons. These are said to make when boiled a refreshing purple drink. So if you get tired of dandelion-and-burdock try crowberry instead, though I should rather think it will take you a long time to collect enough berries—they are so small.

However, these are to be found lower down, on the edge of the summit plateaux. Here cushions of moss campion (*Silene acaulis*) are scattered sparsely—pink jewels, set in the metallic green of leaf and the grey platinum of rock. Dwarf cudweed

(*Gnaphalium supinum*), the little brother of the edelweiss, and starry saxifrage (*Saxifraga stellaris*) are the more conspicuous plants. The rest is moss and lichen: golden-moss at first, among which club-mosses raise their soft green fingers, then blackmoss only as we ascend to the top of Ben Macdhui, which bulges up heavily, wistful and senile, from the eternities of boulder-scree, naked slab and sharp, crunchy grit.

When approached from the north the summit is no more than a big cairn among smaller cairns and the ruins of the sappers' bothies dating from the first survey of the Grampians (see p. 10). Yet, standing at 4,300 feet, Ben Macdhui makes a magnificent viewpoint. Not only does the eye range over the whole of the Cairngorms, but on a clear day it spans the horizons from sea to sea, with crowds of peaks, for identifying which the Cairngorm Club has erected an indicator, bearing directions, names and distances.

The indicator is based on photographic panoramas, which may at times fall short of what the eye can see. This gives rise to a lot of controversy, for instance, about the visibility or otherwise of the Cuillins of Skye, which the indicator does not show. I will leave you to decide whether you can see them or not. I once thought I did . . .

The east is the only side where Ben Macdhui asserts his chieftainship of the Cairngorms with sheer, if badly worn, rock buttresses dropping anything up to 600 feet into the reddish screes of Coire Sputan Dearg (Corrie of Red Spouts). The corrie is a little one-sided. There are no crags on the western slopes of Derry Cairngorm (3,788 feet) to match those of Ben Macdhui, which thrusts out into Glen Luibeg a shoulder, too broad to be a *fiacaill*, though quite ‘ ridgy ’ at the top and craggy on the Sputan side, where a Lochan Uaine—one of the numerous tribe of Green Lochans—sits on a shelf at 3,142 feet. This shoulder of Sròn Riach (Speckled Nose), dividing the Corrie of Red Spouts from the short glen of Allt Càrn a’Mhaim and the ridge of that name above the Lairig, is nowhere of more than light scrambling difficulty and may make an interesting alternative to the more usual routes to or from the big ben.

The upper part of the ridge is quite airy, and, perched high over the Lairig glen, gives a fine view of the great rocky cauldrons of Braeriach and Cairn Toul, with the Devil's Point and Beinn Bhrotain standing, precipitous, farther down the glen against the forests of Deeside. Nearer at hand, Lochan Uaine is straight down at the foot of the crags and the buttresses of Coire Sputan Dearg back up the prospect towards Beinn Mheadhoin, while Derry Cairngorm, though more impressive from the east, raises its handsome cone in the middle distance across the corrie.

The thrills of a ridge walk are rare in the Cairngorms, which makes Sròn Riach and its neighbour Càrn a'Mhaim (a Vam) worthy of notice. The latter stands only 3,329 feet at the highest cairn directly opposite the Devil's Point, but the floor of the intervening glen is below the 2,000-foot contour, which serves to exaggerate the steepness and stature of the Devil's Point (3,303 feet) and Beinn Bhrotain (3,795 feet) beyond the crag-bound entrance to Glen Geusachan. Braeriach and Cairn Toul, if somewhat more distant, are still with us, even though most of Coire Sputan Dearg is now hidden behind Sròn Riach.

The ridge of Càrn a'Mhaim is about three miles long and is linked to Ben Macdhui by a flat saddle, dipping below 2,600 feet at the lowest point. Thus the ridge can be combined with a descent from the big peak along Allt Clach nan Taillear (Burn of the Tailors' Stone) or the bulge between it and Sròn Riach.

The saddle lies within easy compass of Corrour Bothy and could be used to climb Ben Macdhui from this side or, more conveniently, from Glen Luibeg along the course of Allt Càrn a'Mhaim. But the slopes above it involve a steep pull of 1,700 feet. Alternatively you may follow from Glen Luibeg the main stream in Coire Sputan Dearg to a prominent knoll and cross over the ridge on its left (west) to the tourist path from Coire Etchachan. Here the gradients are quite gentle and you can admire the Red Spout cliffs on the way, to be rewarded with views of Loch Etchachan when the ridge is crossed.

Lying at 3,058 feet above sea-level, the loch stays frozen over for some seven months in the year. Yet trout manage to survive in it. As seen from the Macdhui path the loch does not show to advantage. The scene is dominated by the drab and barren hill-tops exposed to the prevailing westerly winds. If you venture, however, over the heaped boulders and rock ribs of its north-western approaches a different sight will meet your eyes.

Protected from the bite of the western and northern gales, and getting a full share of morning and midday sunshine, this side harbours quiet nooks with quick, foaming waters and luscious green sward clinging to the base of the rocks and the abrupt hillsides that plunge into the dark deep. It will be gloriously hot there on a warm summer day, and if you have time to spare you may idle pleasantly on some terraced slabs and watch the trout play and the reflections of the clouds glide over the blue mirror at your feet, or be tempted for a swim in the clear icy water.

Loch Etchachan marks the first break in the eastern half of the horseshoe.

I have nobody's authority for the geological interpretation given below, but it would seem that before the Ice Age Ben Macdhui used to fill Coire Sputan Dearg and even its highest point may have been there. There was neither Loch Etchachan nor anything like the present Coire Etchachan. But a stream was coursing down a gentle gully between Càrn Etchachan and Beinn Mheadhoin into the lakeless narrow V-shaped valley, which now cradles Loch Avon but was then, we may recall (p. 42), part of Strath Nethy.

The climate was warm. Ben Macdhui may have run into a point. And sabre-toothed cats may have come to slake their thirst in the stream after having consumed a hominid or two, ' long time passing '.

The Great Ice came and went, having carried away the pro-truding tors and rounded down the summit of Ben Macdhui. At a later stage two glaciers descended from its chastened heights. One crept towards the Avon glen, to the west of Càrn Etchachan, to join forces with an ice-flow coming from Cairn

Lochan on the line of Garbh Uisge. This caused a big pile-up, which was primarily responsible for the bulldozing of the rocky recess of Loch Avon and the dredging of its deep basin.

Another, smaller ' ice ' followed the pre-Etchachan burn of the sabre-tooths to the same destination, but it could not get into the valley below, as this was already chockful of the first ' ice '. After a bit of an argument between the two, which has given rise to the eastern cliffs of Càrn Etchachan, the second ' ice ' gave up the struggle, and, having obtained a leverage on the hill by sticking an elbow into what has later become the cauldron of Loch Etchachan (not to be confused with Coire Etchachan lower down), it forced its way up the east side of the gully and so over the intervening ridge. There it found another little glen spilling into Glen Derry, which was also blocked by a great flow of ice. The weight of the glacier wore out by and by a rocky gorge in the ridge and so split Derry Cairngorm from Beinn Mheadhoin. Checked in its further progress into Glen Derry, it built up thick, pushing mightily on the sides of the little glen, and so gave it a wide bottle-like outline with a gentle floor of the present Coire Etchachan, the rock scarps and friezes on the sides still bearing witness to the thickness of the ice.

At the same time the wheeling movement in the elbow ground out the bed of Loch Etchachan and smoothed up its enclosing rock bluffs.

Coire Sputan Dearg was already there, or in the making, but at an earlier stage the ice from Ben Macdhui appears to have flowed straight into Glen Derry, high above the level of Coire Etchachan, in a bed, part of which survives in the plateau between Derry Cairngorm (3,788 feet) and the Etchachan ridge of Ben Macdhui.

In the course of time local corrie glaciers and snow-fields alone remained and put finishing touches to the glacial sculpture.

One of these finishing touches is Coire an Lochain Uaine, cradling a tarn of this name, in Derry Cairngorm. This is a true hanging valley, undercut by the Derry glacier. The cliffs of the corrie do not bear comparison with those of its namesake in

Cairn Toul; they are much broken up, except in the north, and the lochan is ' gey wee '. Yet Derry Cairngorm lofts above it in a steep shapely cone, and the corrie has the special charm of a small mountain feature that had once beguiled the professional poacher, philosopher and Gaelic bard William Smith or Gow into building beside the tarn a ' shiel ', which he found ' wondrous warm ' when the hills were ' cauldrife ' with storm and snow.

True, the shiel presented the additional advantage of commanding a wide view of the Forest of Mar, where with the connivance of the Laird of Rothiemurchus he exercised his less artistic talents. After all, not by verse alone will man be alive.

The tourist path gives a wide berth to the little corrie. It follows the Derry Burn from Derry Lodge through a beautiful stretch of unspoiled pinewood to a vast green flat, which certainly was a loch at one time before the burn had ' thirled ' the damming terminal moraine somewhere about the upper footbridge and drained the basin. All that remains of the past magnificence is a tiny lochan at the very foot of the flat, occupying most of middle Glen Derry. Pines straggle thinly on the sides, then give up, but there are plenty of old tree stems embedded in the peat under the heather at the very head of the glen and in Coire Etchachan itself.

The path veers west beyond Glas Allt Mòr and climbs the gentle declivities of the corrie, halfway up which the concrete-and-iron Hutchison Memorial Hut bids an austere welcome to all comers, wearied by the long walk. It also forms a useful base for exploring the surroundings, including the seldom visited peaks of Derry Cairngorm and Beinn Mheadhoin. Both throw up a certain amount of avoidable rock round the edges, but present no difficulty.

Beyond Beinn Mheadhoin the horseshoe is clipped short by upper Glen Avon, and on the Etchachan side of the peak, where the ' second ice ' was halted in its progress, there is a wide stretch of flat ground, cradling a little lochan which drains into Loch Avon. This is another natural gateway to Loch Avon and a crossing from the Hutchison Hut to the Shelter Stone. The middle slopes above Loch Avon are steep, over 200 feet or so, with some incoherent slabby rocks, but of no great account.

Lairig Ghru

CHAPTER SEVEN

Storm in the Lairig Ghru

THE country south of Glen Luibeg and Allt Preas nam Meirleach, which mark the southern boundary of the National Nature Reserve in this part of the Cairngorms, technically belongs to their central division up to Glen Lui and Glen Dee. This, however, is more a matter of topographical convenience than of substance, as the big hills end north of the line. Elsewhere Sgòr Mòr (2,666 feet) and Sgòr Dubh (2,432 feet), the highest points of the heathery uplands between these glens, may have counted for something, but they are reduced to insignificance by the great four-thousanders towering over them north and west.

Thus the beauty of the march glens, except for the uppermost portion of Glen Dee falling within this compass, owes little to their hills and is chiefly one of tree and running water.

Driving roads penetrate the glens as far as the White Bridge over the Dee leading to Glen Geldie where Glen Dee makes an elbow turn to the north and heads for the Lairig Ghru, and all over Glen Lui to Derry Lodge at the foot of Glen Derry and Glen Luibeg, the latter road being barred to traffic by a forest gate, a key to which is obtainable at Mar Lodge. Both roads, however, are right-of-ways as part of the Lairig mounths, and are continued by footpaths. The one up Glen Derry leads to Coire Etchachan and Ben Macdhui, as well as continuing straight on to the Fingalians' Ford on the Avon and eventually Strath Nethy, while a branch track from Derry Lodge connects with

" *Evensong.*" *The **Derry** Forest of the Royal Deeside.*

The Shelter Stone Crag.

Luibeg

the Lairig Ghru path along Allt Preas nam Meirleach, with a further prong of the fork running up Glen Luibeg.

About a quarter of a mile up from the White Bridge the Dee forms a twisting cataract and a beautiful pool, framed by square-cut rocks with trembling aspens. This is the famous Chest of Dee of many paintings. Above the Chest the main interest of the glen lies in the hills ahead, and the five miles to the wide mouth of Glen Geusachan tend to drag. On the way down from the bridge the course of the Dee is enlivened with trees, which gather into woods after two miles or so, at the approaches to the Linn of Dee and the foot of Glen Lui.

The Mar deer are often hand fed in winter and have largely lost their fear of man, so that it is not uncommon to see a group of stags grazing hard by the road and giving no more than a casual look to the passer-by. This is charming, but it is as well to remember that a rutting stag is a potentially dangerous animal. When wild it is too afraid of human beings to attack them, but tame deer sometimes do. A gamekeeper was once killed by his own tame stag. Still, I have never heard of any mishap of this nature in the Forest of Mar.

The Dee washes wide and placid enough down its granite bed, but about half-a-mile short of Glen Lui it has come upon a band of hard, obdurate schist, in which it has worn out a narrow, sinuous channel known as the Linn of Dee. When in spate, the river forcing its way through the cleft makes an impressive sight. The throb of its waters can be clearly felt in the solid masonry of the bridge spanning the Linn, and the thunderous roar can be heard for miles around.

Before the war the forest extended unbroken to Braemar along the lower slopes and thronged thickly up Glen Lui, but most of it has fallen to the lumberer's axe and tractor. Even so, enough trees remain along the Lui Water to preserve some of its original character. It is a beautiful water-course. Livelier than the Dee, the Lui stream foams over rocky steps and goes into deep green-blue pools, a fitting guide to the high bens.

E

Lui was once a populous glen, but it was cleared of crofters involved in the Jacobite rising of 1715 by the successors of the luckless Earl of Mar, and only low overgrown dykes with foxgloves among the grass still bear witness to the past.

At the Derry and its lodge the water forks into Luibeg and Glen Derry. The lower Glen Luibeg, between Càrn Crom (2,847 feet), a southern outlier of Derry Cairngorm, with a corrie bearing the romantic name of Coire Craobh an Oir, Corrie of the Tree of Gold, and Sgòr Dubh, which rises quite steeply over Luibeg Cottage, is wooded on both sides. Scattered firs climb the hillsides and follow the Luibeg Burn towards Allt Preas nam Meirleach.

I remember the place in the slanting morning and evening sunshine, with long shadows, the grass plated gold, the sky without a cloud, and that great stillness that sometimes comes upon the hills and feels almost holy.

It was not quite so on a certain morning when I set out in the company of a Manchester schoolmaster from Luibeg Cottage for the Lairig Ghru by the way of Preas nam Meirleach. I was so tired of carrying heavy weights that I had jumped, all too readily it proved, at the opportunity of sending off by post from Braemar everything I thought I could spare, including my oilskin cape.

The weather certainly looked set fair. The day before had been brimful with sunshine, painting streaks of glowing verdure among the pines of Sgòr Dubh above the keeper's cottage. The smoke had risen from the ' lum ' in a straight blue column, and the water had folded small, like translucent silk, in the burn's elbow by the bridge. But when, next morning, we took the high road at 8.45 D.S.T., which is 6.45 a.m. by God's own clock, after a generous breakfast, grey downy clouds were obscuring the hills and the air was sultry and heavy, though cool.

My companion was wearing grey flannels and ordinary ' walking shoes '—an attire not to be recommended for this crossing—and the size of his rucksack was an undisclosed multiple of mine. Accordingly, I offered to have as many rests on the way as he thought fit, and the first of these took place soon after we had surmounted the initial rise of Càrn a'Mhaim. The path along Allt Preas nam Meirleach was somewhat peaty, but mercifully dry. Beinn Bhrotain showed ahead as a low grey wall, decapitated by cloud.

Some twenty minutes later we were in Glen Dee, where a group of walkers, overtaken by the night, were just beginning to stir in an overcrowded tent. There was some exchange of opinions about the exact location of Corrour Bothy, which was very difficult to spot—a large grey boulder among many smaller grey boulders. And the sun was not shining on the heap of rusty tins to lend colour to the scene! In my superior wisdom I poked a finger at a belt of peat-hags and, as I later had occasion to discover, missed the bothy by some fifty yards.

A few blaeberries, gleaned on the way, had further delayed us. Nevertheless we were making good progress, and this part of the path was comfortable enough. Above, on our right, battalions of mists were retreating in fleecy curls into the black rocks of Càrn a'Mhaim. The Geusachan heights, the Devil's Point and Cairn Toul were pale-slate in the uncertain light. Thunder was growling distantly among the hills, but there seemed to be no direct imminence of a storm, and for all one could see it might yet clear up.

At 11.30 (D.S.T.) we passed the boulder by which, according to tradition, three tailors had died one Hogmanay night on their way to a dance in Braemar (see p. 12), and an hour later we sat down to lunch above the first step of the Lairig Pass, roughly half-a-mile short of the Pools of Dee.

Thrown into relief by the misty background, the Angel's Peak showed to advantage the steep angle of its north face. Cairn Toul was clear. Above the swish of falling waters, great stillness reigned among the hazy bens. Grey clouds were crawling sluggishly over the western summits. A few desultory drops of moisture fell from the sky. Then, suddenly, without any apparent reason, lead-blue dusk overflowed the corries. The sky above Cairn Toul darkened, a red lightning wreathed its top and a peal of rasping thunder rolled from rock to rock. I looked up.

Steely phantoms were spilling over Braeriach in rapid lasso loops. It grew darker and darker, as though it were a solar eclipse. The path showed dimly, the stones glinting, pale in the twilight. A ghostly whiteness bulged out over the cliff-sweep of the Rough Corrie, toppled over and began to advance, quickly obliterating the view.

The storm appeared to be moving at a tangent, and we ran fast up the path in the hope of getting out of its way; but we had made little headway before lightning came splashing and crackling on the brows of Braeriach and Ben Macdhui, which hemmed in, lowly, the broad pass, and a straight heavy rain rushed upon us down the westward hillsides. I thought it prudent to retreat into the deep ravine of the Dee and await developments there. We huddled to the streaming bank with rucksacks on our heads, as hail and water enclosed us with white impenetrable walls and thunder roared, crashed and hissed on all sides. Soon the stream at our feet swelled into a raging torrent, rocking the ground with its pulse.

In a few minutes I was soaked to the skin, my only protection being the thinness of my parachute-silk anorak and sleeveless tennis shirt, which were glued tight to my body. My companion did not fare much better, despite his raincoat.

After a quarter of an hour or so the downpour eased off slightly, and, having little to lose, we decided to go on. We passed the first, larger Pool of Dee, and then the second, a mere puddle amidst a scree-field. To me it was like a nightmarish Regent Street during the blitz before the all-clear—a mixture of magnificence, make-believe and vaguely apprehended danger. The boulders hissed wickedly with ' silent ' electric discharges, and left and right wavering fiery threads connected to rock outcrops. I instinctively accelerated my pace on the high open stretches of the path, to slow down again in the harmless hollows. In his townie shoes and awkward coat, my companion was bravely keeping up with me, as I danced over heaped boulders in a mood of battle hilarity.

We passed several false summits, produced by moraines and scree slides, under which the Lairig burns often disappear, giving the impression of flowing uphill, and, amid a new onslaught of the storm, reached the two large cairns, marking the topmost point of the pass at 2,733 feet. Four men who had been coming up from the Aviemore side had turned back and were now leading the way, a few hundred yards in front of us. There were more people farther down the glen.

Our hair was pasted to our heads in thin wet wisps and water came streaming down the tips of our noses. I kept blowing at mine, to head the stream off my open neck, with moderate success. My thick climbing breeches weighed like a suit of armour.

As we emerged from the defile on to the wider lower terrace of the Lairig glen, a hoary tumult broke loose above the cone of Càrn Eilrig and dispersed in flocks of cotton-wool over the blue Strathspey. The sky brightened up behind the Sgorans, and gradually a white ragged veil displaced the massed nimbus and the sun came seeping through. Soon after, the rain stopped, enabling us to take off and wring out some of our clothes and spread our shirts and jackets on a large cairn (no Memorial Hut then), where they dried quickly in the brisk breeze and sunshine, while we munched our ' pieces '. There was literally not a dry patch left on me, and I squeezed pints of water out of my luckless breeches; but, fortunately, the depths of my rucksack contained a dry sweater and a scarf with which to cover my chilly nakedness.

At 3 p.m. (D.S.T.) we gathered our belongings and hurried on to Coylumbridge, to catch the bus to Aviemore, which we did easily enough. Two more showers passed over us on our way, and, while sheltering during one of these under the pines of Blackpark, we heard a short sharp report as though of a field gun fired as a tree was struck by lightning somewhere in the neighbourhood.

At Aviemore I said goodbye to my companion and ducked into ' Pot Luck ' for high tea. White cloudlets spread a fleecy mantle over the round shoulders of Braeriach and mist refilled the V-gap of the Lairig Ghru.

This was a considerable rain- and thunder-storm and, I believe, caused some flooding of the Dee, to which this river is prone, though not nearly so catastrophic as that of August 1829, of which Sir Dick Lauder has left us an eyewitness account.

He writes:—

" During the afternoon the wind and rain gradually increased, and about 5 o'clock it blew a perfect hurricane, driving clouds of rain before it, somewhat resembling snow-drift. It was during one of these violent gusts of wind that the first flash of lightning occurred. It was intensely vivid, and then followed peal after peal of thunder, not of the rolling kind, but ' as if whole batteries of the pieces of Heaven's ordnance had been discharged in rapid succession.' About 7 o'clock in the evening the thunder ceased, but the wind and rain continued, and many of the smaller streams, already swollen, commenced their havoc. Shocks of earthquake were felt at Allanquoich, and at Crathie, three of Dr. Robertson's men-servants, who were sleeping in a loft, started from their beds, felt the house shake, and heard a noise as if the slates were falling off the roof. The combined horrors of this dreadful night led many people in Braemar to imagine that the end of the world was approaching.

The Dee reached its height at different places in Braemar between the hours of 8 and 10 in the morning of the 4th. By correct measurements by Dr. Robertson, at six different points of the river, the average breadths of which was 130 feet, the mean rise of the whole was 15 to 16 feet."*

In the age of atomic bombs and spaceflight it would take a lot to make people imagine that the end of the world was approaching. Still, that must have been quite a storm, and it is left to us to picture what it was like then in the Lairig Ghru.

In more recent times serious floods of the Dee occurred in 1914 and 1920.

---

* Quoted after *Crathie and Braemar* by Rev. John Stirton, p. 372.

CHAPTER EIGHT

In and About Glen More

GLEN More, the Great Glen of the Cairngorms, is no ordinary valley. It is broad and wedge-shaped, as though a part of Strathspey pushed in between the Kincardine Hills and the Cairngorms proper. Between its apex in the Pass of Ryvoan and the foot of Loch Morlich, Glen More is an unmistakable entity, but beyond the loch it merges imperceptibly into the glacial driftlands of Rothiemurchus, and the boundary between them is proprietary rather than geographical.

While Rothiemurchus was a Grant domain, Glen More belonged to the vast estates of the Earls of Huntly, later created Dukes of Gordon, and so it remained until it was acquired in 1923 by the Forestry Commission. Reafforestation ensued, for the ancient Glenmore Forest had been repeatedly felled from the seventeenth century onwards, chiefly in connection with the successive great wars, starting with Napoleon, and was in the main left to its own devices, to recoup its losses. It was also called upon to supply its share of 40,000 cubic feet of timber in the last war under a more scientific management, as well as suffering accidental damage by fire. Thus, most of the present forest is young, dating from 1924 or later, with Sitka and Norway spruces added to the indigenous Scots pine. It was named the Queen's Forest in honour of Queen Mary on the occasion of the Silver Jubilee in 1935.

As the Earls of Huntly were ' created ' Dukes of Gordon, so

was the Forestry Commission estate in Glen More 'created' National Forest Park in 1948. The primary object of a forest park is forestry, but land above 1,700 feet is not generally suitable for afforestation, and as the Park boundary runs along the confining ridges it does take in a good deal of intervening high ground.

Apart from its utilitarian purpose, any National Forest Park is a national playground and so open to the public, subject to such restriction as the considerations of rational forestry may require. The restrictions affect mainly young plantings and making fires or smoking in the afforested areas. Camping is also restricted for the same reason and special grounds for camping and caravanning have been provided on the alluvial flats at the head of Loch Morlich. Indeed, the Park has been greatly developed as a recreational area since the date of its initiation, more particularly for ski-ing. But the road to Coire Cas and the chair-lift on Cairn Gorm, if not the ski-tows, can also be used in summer, thus affording an easy way of reaching the High Tops, which otherwise involves a good deal of toil and moil, and will absorb about two hours in climbing time. The S.C.P.R. Glenmore Lodge and the Youth Hostel also add to the possibilities of Glenmore as a base right at the foot of the high peaks.

The Rothiemurchus Hut, although technically just outside the Park area, may be regarded as still within the geographical Glen More. The hut stands on the lower slopes of Castle Hill (2,366 feet), the first summit in the eastern border ridge of the Lairig Ghru, conveniently at the entrance to this defile, and is connected by a forest road with the foot of Loch Morlich.

Castle Hill steepens up abruptly about a hundred yards above the hut, where the drift deposits give way to the glacier-worn slopes. By itself the hill is of no great account, but it forms the first step of the ridge walk to the Lurcher's Crag, or Creag an Leth-choin (3,448 feet), which rises proudly above the Lairig Ghru and is conspicuous from Aviemore. Before, however, we can reach it from Castle Hill we have to cross another little summit, called Creag a'Chalamain or Pigeons' Crag (2,579 feet).

This heaves up quietly in the north, to end up abruptly in a 'clatter' of rocks, overlooking the col that makes a prominent notch in the Glenmore skyline. A geologist will recognize in the col a dry overflow channel, formed at the time when an ice-dammed lake filled part of the Lairig Ghru. The shelving moors above Glen More were also under water, ponded back by the piedmont glacier below. The little Lochan Dubh a'Chadha to the north-east of the knob of Argiod-meall (Hill of Silver, 2,118 feet) may be described, with some stretch of imagination, as the last remnant of that Ice-Age lake.

Be this as it may, a walking path from Glenmore to the Lairig crosses the crag-bound 'notch'. The path branches off the Coire Cas road a little above the bridge and is carried over Allt Mòr by a footbridge beside a bothy, approximately in line with the road hairpins and the large glacial erratic known as Clach Bharraig. It leads straight to the Sinclair Memorial Hut in the Lairig Ghru.

The a'Chalamain rocks, although used for climbing practice by the S.C.P.R. classes, are not high and can readily be by-passed. Beyond the 'notch' the Lurcher's Crag builds up steeply but uneventfully over 1,000 feet to its lower summit of 3,365 feet. Henceforth the ridge continues gentle, though encumbered with large boulders on the farther side of the main cairn (3,448 feet), perched on the brink of a precipice. The peak sweeps away towards Glen More in long heathery slopes, but breaks off towards the Lairig in rock ribs and buttresses up to some 300 feet high, which are continued by steep screes. The rocks may not be of any great climbing account, but they make an impressive sight, and the peak commands wide views of the Lairig Ghru and Coire an Lochain, with the tarn and a stretch of green sward where deer often graze.

Beyond the summit there is an expanse of gentle ground known as the Lurcher's Crag Meadow, from which the white ribbon of Allt Creag an Leth-choin and a path lead to Glen More, while a deer track threads its way to the lochan, where the walking path can be joined at a higher level. At the time of writing, the little Jean's Hut, originally in Coire Cas, is being re-erected in Coire an Lochain. The hut, which contains mountain rescue equipment, is locked and the key is obtainable at Glenmore Lodge. If you have enough energy left the ascent may be continued to Ben Macdhui or Cairn Gorm, which are roughly equidistant. Or else you may feel like crossing over the lower spur of Fiacaill a'Choire an t'Sneachda to that corrie, which cradles two small lochans among piled boulders. It is more rocky than Coire an Lochain, but lacks its green flat and wears an empty, wind- and echo-haunted look. Cloudberry (*Rubus chamaemorus*) is quite plentiful on the sides. The plant is related to raspberry, but does not look much like it, and bears white flowers which resemble anemones made of crumpled cloth and sometimes result in tasty peach-coloured fruits.

The next fiacaill, though steep on the sides, is not difficult and may be used to climb to the top of Cairn Gorm, or to come down from it to Coire Cas and the White Lady Shieling. Coire Cas, however, is of little interest, except to a skier in winter, and Cairn Gorm can be reached more easily by the chair-lift which ends up some 500 feet below the crowning dome of the peak. At least one well-worn path leads up to the summit cairn. If, though, you disdain mechanical aids, you may follow the old walking path up the Aonach shoulder (Sròn an Aonaich) from Clach Bharraig, which is easy but quite a grind.

The summit offers fine views of Speyside, with the Queen's Forest and Loch Morlich for a foreground, but the Cairngorms do not appear to their best advantage. The back of Ben Macdhui is not very inspiring, and the Lochs, Avon and Etchachan, gleam thinly among their crags. Beyond the studded whaleback of Beinn Mheadhoin the Eastern Cairngorms sprawl in flattish brown panoramas. The only show of precipice and cliff is nearer at hand in the Snowy Corrie and its fiacaill, but even these are seen at an oblique angle.

There are 8 miles of pleasant walking between Cairn Gorm and Ryvoan. The ridge ramble may be taken up or down, though the latter is easier if you use the chair-lift—and so past

Marquis' Well, a remarkable spring only 100 feet or so below the summit, over Cnap Coire na Spreidhe (Crap Corrie na Sprey), to the edge of the small cliffs of Coire Laoigh Mòr (Corrie Lui More), and another flight of rocks, called Stac na h-Iolaire (Stack na Heelar), which may be rendered as Eagle's Point, in the side of Màm Suim (2,409 feet), quite a handsome little peak, linked by a lowly col to the last outpost of the ridge, Creag nan Gall (Foreigners' Crag, 2,040 feet), above Ryvoan.

Creag nan Gall drops away steeply towards the pass in heather slopes, a frieze of rock and piled boulder-screes rimmed with Scots firs, the difference of levels being about 800 feet. At its foot nestles the greenest of all Green Lochans, the Lochan Uaine of Ryvoan. The colour effect may be partly due to the contrast with the reddish screes, partly to the reflections of the pines, but legend will have as its main cause that the 'wee folk', who are given to the wearing of the green, use the lochan for washing their clothes.

Ryvoan, or Rebhoan, is another example of glacial overflow, and Creag nan Gall's rocks are matched by the scarp of Creag Loisgte (Loysht, Burnt Crag) across the pass. This carries a forest track connecting Nethybridge with Glen More. It follows the old Rathad nam Meirleach, the Thieves' Road, and is, therefore, a right-of-way. It was, in fact, much used by Loch-aber cattle reivers to get away with their loot from Rothie-murchus and Glen More, and has been the scene of some skir-mishes between them and their pursuers. The wide view of Glen More the pass commands was, no doubt, used to advantage by the reivers. Times have changed, but the view is still there, and Ryvoan, which is only a couple of miles beyond Glenmore Lodge, is well worth a visit.

The Cairn Gorm-Creag nan Gall ridge borders on the deep, narrow glen of Strath Nethy. The confining glacial slopes are steep, and the glen runs straight, almost due north and south, from the Saddle above Loch Avon to the footbridge on the Nethy carrying the Lairig an Lui path over the river beside a derelict bothy—a distance of about 5½ miles. A heather track threads its thin way beside Garbh Allt, the main headwater of the Nethy rising on the Saddle.

There is a rock frieze on both sides of the glen, especially the west, but it is mostly fragmentary and discontinuous. The face of Cairn Gorm is very steep in the lower glacial profile above the Saddle. There is no rock scarp here, however, and the descent, though not a walk and requiring adequate mountaineering footwear, is not even a scramble, and may serve as an introduction to a traverse of the hills beyond Strath Nethy.

These are seldom visited, but not inconsiderable. To begin with, A'Choinneach swells up gradually into a flattish plateau, which is a favourite haunt of deer herds and has its highest point 738 feet above the saddle. Though not a great peak, A'Chòinneach offers interesting views of the surroundings of Loch Avon, with Cairn Gorm and Beinn Mheadhion flanking the recess. Ahead, in the north, Bynack More or Ben Bynack lofts up to 3,574 feet in a handsome cone beyond a dip in the summit plateau, involving a drop of some 300 feet from the summit cairn of A'Chòinneach.

More, which has a minor companion summit in the north-west referred to as Bynack Beg, the two jointly being ' The Bynacks ', is steepish on all sides, especially in the east, where it sports an interesting cluster of tors known as the Barns of Bynack. It forms a mile-long ridge, with some crag and boulder-scree, in its upper part.

I remember passing that way one grey day and an eagle circling slowly above the ridge until eventually it veered away towards Bynack Beg. You may see it, too, or else you may not, " I cannot be positive which."

The descent to Ryvoan presents no difficulty.

More adventurously you may strike the forest track about 100 yards beyond Glenmore Lodge, follow it to the foot of Màm Suim, and thence the burn to the col, cross this over to the corrie of Stac na h-Iolaire and so by easy slopes to Strath Nethy. The ground here may be rather wet and the burn difficult to cross, so that it will probably pay to contour the slopes for about a mile up the glen to Allt a'Choire Dheirg, taking the latter as a guide to Bynack More. The Red Corrie (Coire Deirg) itself has some fine cliffs on the sides, but these fail to close over the gentle declivities at the head along the burn.

Incidentally, the El Alamein Refuge is located in the ridge of Cairn Gorm above Strath Nethy at the head of a gully to the north of Cnap Coire na Spreidhe. Its siting has often been criticized, and, indeed, it does seem that it could have been more useful elsewhere.

The area of Loch Morlich and the forest and moor tracks between the Kincardines and the Lairig Ghru afford a variety of less exacting low-level rambles. The walks to the Slugan and Ryvoan passes suggest themselves naturally. The first of these is wholly and the second partly accessible to wheeled transport, to which ordinary forest roads are closed. Red and roe deer, quite plentiful in these parts, are excluded from the forest by the deer fence, in which stiles are provided, but they roam freely on the moors beyond. Reindeer, once indigenous to the Highlands, disappeared sometime in the thirteenth century, but were reintroduced from Sweden in several stages in 1952 and have now become established in Glen More under the auspices of the Reindeer Company Ltd.

Capercailzie, the largest of the grouse, had similarly to be restocked from Sweden at an earlier date and may now be seen in the forests of Glen More and Rothiemurchus, together with blackcock and red grouse. An interesting bird, wholly confined to this district and now sadly reduced in numbers, is the charming crested tit. Oyster-catchers will be heard shrilling above Loch Morlich, also frequented by sandpipers and goosanders. In addition to the *iolaire dubh*, which is our golden eagle called " black " in Gaelic after the underside of its wings, the peregrine falcon is no stranger to Glen More, though the jealously guarded osprey is to be found only in Abernethy Forest five miles north of the Kincardines.

Of the furry predators pine marten, once common, is now extinct in this part of Scotland, but fox, badger and wild cat are not. In fact, the wild-cat population of the Highlands has been largely concentrated here owing to the felling of extensive tracts of forest during the war.

The Scottish wild cat is not to be confused with feral cats, in other words domestic cats gone wild; it is a different species, much larger and readily distinguishable by its broad bushy tail with black and white rings, ending in a ' ball ' instead of a point. Some of the taxidermists' specimens I have seen had large heads and a tabby pattern, but the cat I saw killed by a car had long legs, a little like a cheetah, uniform greyish-brown body fur, resembling a common hare's, and a head small in proportion to its size.

In whichever guise it may appear, it is well to heed the MacPherson motto " Touch not the cat but the glove," for it is a bundle of ferocity which will not hesitate to attack a man if cornered or provoked—and the decision of what constitutes provocation is entirely up to the cat.

It is, however, a nocturnal animal, and only once did I see a wild cat in the open, running up a hillside about 100 yards away in Glen Feshie. But I have smelled cats in Rothiemurchus.

The road over An Slugan connects Loch Morlich with Boat of Garten. I spent one summer in the latter village and often crossed this pass on my way to the hills. One unforgettable experience was a sunrise on the Cairngorms, seen from An Slugan. Its highest point is almost exactly 1,000 feet a.s.l., but the road climbs higher up the southern slopes of the Kincardine Hills on the way to Loch Morlich.

These slopes are gradual, thickly-coated with glacial drift about three-quarters of the way up to the top, and while receiving the warmth and moisture of the south-western winds sheltered by the Kincardines from the north and the Cairngorms proper from the east. This creates conditions very favourable to the growth of trees, which ascend in places as high as the 1,800-foot contour. Above the tree-line the hills are heather-grown, with a few schist hummocks or felsite dykes sticking out like knuckle-bones at the summit edges. The whole range from Ryvoan to

Loch Pityoulish is about six miles long and, taken either way, makes a pleasant airy walk with wide views of the Cairngorms and Speyside and without much climbing on the way, except at the two ends.

Meall a'Bhuachaille (Myall a Voohal, meaning the Shepherd's Hill), the highest of the Kincardines (2,654 feet), is a shapely cone and a prominent landmark of Glen More. There is a path running along a burn from the back of the Youth Hostel to the col between this hill and its neighbour, Creagan Gorm (2,403 feet), which makes the easiest approach to the summit. Above Ryvoan the Meall is quite steep, though less so on the Nethy side of the pass, and, since the difference of levels is about 1,200 feet, this is a fairly stiff pull. The descent to the col involves a drop of some 600 feet, followed by a rise of 400 to Creagan Gorm. Henceforth our route continues to Craiggowrie (2,237 feet) without much change in altitude. The latter is a pleasant hummocky hill, wine-red with bell heather in the summer, above the Slugan pass, a descent to which may be made along the deer fence marking the march of the Glenmore Forest Park. The drop is some 1,200 feet over gradual slopes.

Beyond the Slugan there are two more hummocky heights: the wooded Creag Ghreusache (1,416 feet) and the bare-headed Creag Chaisteal (1,465 feet), the last of the Cairngorms, whose low elevation is partly offset by the proximity of the Spey, over which it yet rises sharply enough some 800 feet, and the loch at its foot. The summit is the site of an ancient Pictish fort, whence the name Creag Chaisteal—the Castle Crag. The lower slopes are grown with birch and pine, and have a distinct glacial shelf, perched like a raised beach over the water.

Loch Pityoulish is shallow and reedy in the south, where at high water it claims some marshy ground, the haunts of wild duck and greylag geese; but at the north end it attains 74 feet. It is said to contain an artificial island with remnants of primitive fortifications, which emerges at low water.

Thus the place lacks neither scenic nor archaeological interest, but to me Creag Chaisteal is above all a kind of scale model of the Cairngorms, containing within its small compass samples of every type of country found among them. Birchwoods come half-way up the slopes. Higher up some old pines stand, spaced over a steep moss-grown incline, and grassy hollows are contained by slanting rock ribs that will yield good 'bouldering' practice to a climber. Then it is heather and peat-hags, among which small sheets of water sit, scattered with white puffs of cotton-grass. In the summer you will find wild strawberries disputing possession of the small patches of soil ensconced in the rocks with bell-heather and rock-rose, alpine lady's-mantle, needle-whin, milkwort and stray foxgloves.

Perhaps you have not the same feeling as I for such small 'cuddly mountains', but if you like to shed a tear over "the old unhappy things and battles long ago" you may go to the other side of the loch. Here the low Calart Hill has a hollow where blaeberries grow sweet over the earthly remains of the Cummings treacherously slain by the Shaws in 1396. Or, for a more recent sorrow, a round dyke at the head of the loch en-closes a little graveyard of the Ogilvies of Elgin, where a young man and his sweetheart, killed in a climbing accident on the black rocks of the Sgorans (if memory serves, in 1924), were laid to rest. When I was there the deep blue of autumn gentians in the yellowing grass remembered their mountain love . . . But tread softly—it is private.

Glen More and Meall a' Bhuachaille.

CHAPTER NINE

The Great Moss and the Bens of the West

CONTAINED between Strathspey and Glen Geldie north and south, and between the Lairig Ghru and Glen Feshie east and west, the Western Cairngorms form a solid block of high country, which illustrates better than any other part of these mountains their geological ancestry in an uplifted tableland, dismembered by erosion. This block is based on the 40-square-mile expanse of the Great Moss (Am Moine Mhòr), which does not sink much below 3,000 feet at any point and whose upraised rims provide the main summits. The original plateau has been encroached upon round the edges by the existing streams and vanished glaciers, more particularly in the north and east, where Gleann Einich, the corries of Braeriach and Glen Geusachan have broken it into promontories and ridges, all of which, however, still adhere closely to the Great Moss.

The latter is a unique feature. Less barren than the stony uplands of Ben Macdhui and Cairn Lochan, it stretches in a wistful dun-grey tundra, over which mists are driven by the south wind that will lash you with blinding rain in the summer and biting ice spicules in the winter, bleak yet not without a peculiar charm of its own.

Despite the name, there is not much moss there, except possibly on the west rim. Most of the area is grown with sedges and rushes, which, grey-yellow and red-brown in the autumn, match to perfection the coats of the red deer that gather among

F*

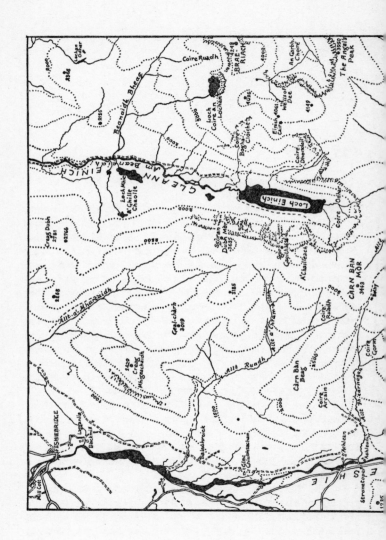

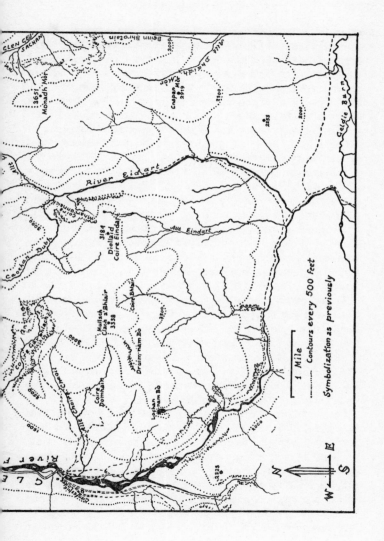

1 Mile

------ Contours every 500 feet

Symbolization as previously

them in the rutting season. The Great Moss has a general southward dip and its three main burns, Caochan Dubh, Allt Sgairnich and Allt Luineag, fall into the Eidart, an original tributary of the Geldie captured by the Feshie in its headward erosion. The glen of the Eidart with a small rock-rimmed Coire Mharconaich at its head reduces the central north-to-south span of the Moss to about a mile and a half, and a-thousand-feet-deep, isolates between it and Glen Geusachan the peaks of Monadh Mòr (3,651 feet) and Beinn Bhrotain (3,795 feet) into a distinct massif, sometimes referred to as the Southern Cairngorms. A stalking path runs up the Eidart to a point half-a-mile short of Coire Mharconaich and so fails to contact another stalking path which leads from Glen Feshie over Càrn Bàn Mòr and peters out in the middle course of Allt Sgairnich.

The upper reaches of this stream have been churned up into a sea of peat-hags, over which strips and sickles of land grown with sedge, cloudberry and rush still rise in places. Waders thrive here, but, unless frozen, such ground is a nightmare to the walker.

The central portion of the Great Moss between the gap of the Eidart and the wider gulf of Loch Einich is a country of glacial knolls, the geologist's *roches moutonnées*. In a hollow among these sits Loch nan Cnapan (pr. Crapan), the Lake of the Knolls. This is a welcome landmark on a misty day among a featureless and repetitive waste. The loch issues in a burn which tumbles down towards Loch Einich over the precipitous head of Coire Odhar (Our), about a mile to the north.

Between Loch nan Cnapan, the rim of Coire Odhar and the lower rise of Braeriach, which heaves up insignificantly in a low dome above the Great Moss, extends a miniature lakeland, made up of rock ribs, ice-smoothed hummocks, winding watercourses and a multitude of unnamed and unmapped tarns, ranging in size from mere pools, though often quite deep, to substantial lochans, not much smaller than Loch nan Cnapan itself. This is a country to be avoided if you are in a hurry or have designs on the high peaks. So keep well south of Loch nan

Cnapan until you reach a prominent knoll (3,009 feet) midway between Allt Sgairnich and Allt Luineag, where the march cairns of the 'Forests' of Glen Feshie, Rothiemurchus and Mar converge. This is a handy point, whence you may strike off north-west for Braeriach and Cairn Toul, or follow the depression of Allt Luineag between these and Monadh Mòr for about a mile to Loch nan Stuirteag (Loch of Black-headed Gulls), sitting at 2,840 feet on a shelf above Glen Geusachan, which is yours if you keep to the downward course of the burn flowing from the loch.

If, however, the day is fine and you have no burning schemes on your mind, you may as well spend a quiet hour among the rocky intricacies of the little lakeland, with its patches of sweet grass, hemmed in among boulders, bare slabs of clean granite, rills, water-filled hollows and glistening tarns. In the distance, beyond the hidden gap of Coire Odhar, the dark Sgorans rise menacingly, but here all is peace in the chaste solitude. The deer will be with you, the white-winged ptarmigan and the plovers' plaints. And if you venture to the edge of the cliffs in which the Great Moss breaks off towards Loch Einich a mighty Alpine view will rush upon you.

On your left are the Sgorans, 2,000 feet of rock and scree, ribbed with steep ridges, with a green hollow of Coire nan Eichan (Horses' Corrie), where deer often graze and into which an indistinct path zig-zags down from Càrn Bàn Mòr, tucked up in a corner. Observe a pinnacle in the first ridge. At some angles it looks like a hooded figure with bowed head and hands folded in prayer. But do not be deceived by these pious appearances, for this is A'Chailleach, the Witch of Lynchat turned to stone, and in Gaelic lore she casts an evil spell over the loch.

Facing her in the crags of Braeriach stands another, smaller pinnacle—Am Bodach, the Old Man. He is a benevolent personage, whose protection you may seek from the wiles of A'Chailleach (the Old Woman), but, alas! his powers are not up to hers, so that if in doubt keep to the Braeriach side of Loch Einich—it is safer. When nobody is looking the two are said

to 'put boulders' at each other across the mile-wide gap
by way of connubial argument.

The crag frieze of Coire Odhar is broken up at several points
where a descent to Loch Einich can be made over scree-shoots,
best on the west side, A'Chailleach notwithstanding.

On your right, beyond Am Bodach, the slopes of Braeriach
form a shelf at the familiar 3,250-foot contour. The line of the
shelf is continued over Loch Einich by a ridge, rocky on the west
side and about a mile long. This is the outside rim of the two-
lobed Coire Dhondail (pr. Ghowntal). The corrie is surmounted by a low rock frieze, much broken up about the middle
where a path, fragmentary above the corrie, descends to Gleann
Einich, to the charred ruin of John of Corrour's Bothy, which
used always to be provided with some meal for benighted
travellers. Beyond this point a rough forest road runs along the
river Bennie (Am Benaidh) to Tullochgrue and so to Aviemore,
10 miles away. It may be possible to cover part of this stretch by
car, but many people who climb Braeriach by this route or
some other variant from Gleann Einich find a bicycle useful,
especially on the return. I know, however, of at least one case
where the bicycle could not be found, having been 'borrowed'
by a person unknown.

There is some crag in Coire Bogha-cloiche above the lower
end of Loch Einich, but the sidings of Braeriach between the
head of Coire Dhondail and Coire Lochain in the north, though
steep, present no more formidable obstacle to the foot than
extensive fields of boulder-scree. Apart from the already-
mentioned path, the easiest approach from this side is by the
slopes west of Coire Lochain. The gradients ease off at 3,800
feet or so, to turn 100 feet higher up into a plateau, rather flatter
than anything on Ben Macdhui. Above the Great Moss the
plateau swells into the South Top of Braeriach (4,149 feet).

Three-quarters of a mile to the north-north-west is the Einich
Cairn (4,061 feet), a hardly perceptible prominence dignified for
some obscure reason with big print in the O.S. Tourist Map.
The plateau is enlivened with occasional cushions of moss

campion and small oases of sedge and rush (*Juncus trifidus*) and, perhaps oddly, stunted plants of blaeberry. Golden-moss, seldom golden save in a wet summer, and black-moss, ranging in colour from bright yellow to Indian ink, but almost pure purple in June and July, line the trickling rills which gather in the ill-defined hollow about the middle of Braeriach's upland. Here two fairly copious streams bubble up from a number of springs, known as the Wells of Dee, and pursue their course in rocky beds to the edge of the great rock cauldron of An Garbh Choire Mòr, the Great Rough Corrie of Braeriach, plunging over it in a thin waterfall of impressive height.

This lobe of the Great Rough Corrie is known as Garbh Choire Dhàidh (Garra Horrie Yay, Rough Corrie of the Dee) and bounded by slabby rock buttresses, those " grisly cliffs that guard the infant rills of Highland Dee." These were climbed in 1810 by Dr. George Keith Skene in the first recorded rock climb ever made in the Cairngorms.

The Great Rough Corrie is 1½ miles across between the waterfall of the Dee and the rocky spur of the Angel's Peak, or Sgòr an Lochain Uaine (3,950 feet), in the south, and is undoubtedly the corrie of all Cairngorm corries. It is the seat of a crescent of semi-eternal snow and, according to tradition, the lair of a She Devil, who presumably is " more deadly than the male." About a quarter of a mile east of the waterfall the rocks peter out and the ground swells towards the highest point of Braeriach (4,248 feet) directly above the main rock face of Coire Bhrochain (Vrohan).

The green lace of alpine lady's mantle graces the dark buttresses of the corrie, some of which attain 800 feet above the scree and in which mists are often caught and come up swirling like the steam rising from a porridge pot, whence apparently the name— the Porridge Corrie, though other etymologies have been suggested. Cairn Toul (4,241 feet) lofts up airily across the two-mile-wide, 2,000-foot-deep gap and Lochain Uaine, perched on the glacial shelf of Coire an Lochain Uaine, sets off the stern scene of rock and scree.

Between Coire Bhrochain in the south and Coire Beanaidh in the north Braeriach has been worn down to a ridge, narrow by Cairngorm standards, which leads eastwards to a col, carrying the usual route and a kind of path to the Pools of Dee. Alternatively you may continue, with little effort, north to the flat-topped Sròn na Lairig (3,875 feet) and descend to the highest point (2,733 feet) of the Lairig pass, or else to Coire Gorm in the north, whence both the Sinclair Memorial Hut and Gleann Einich can be reached without difficulty over sweeping heathery inclines. The same routes can, of course, be tackled in reverse and some variants are possible, but it must be borne in mind that farther down the Lairig Ghru Sròn na Lairig is undercut by a rocky scarp of considerable height and steepness.

The north side of Braeriach is scooped out into three shapely corries, conspicuous from Aviemore. The westernmost of these, Coire Lochain, cradles a tarn, called tautologously Loch Coire an Lochain and filling almost its entire breadth. The semi-circle of cliffs stooping over the loch may be not as impressive as the black precipices of Coire Bhrochain or An Garbh Choire Mòr; still it is some 200 feet high, and in combination with the green-blue water and the steep banks of snow which often last here well into the summer it makes a fine sight. The next two corries, Coire Ruadh (the Red Corrie) and Coire Beanaidh (Corrie of the Bennie) have hardly any ' live rock ' left, and their steep scarps are composed almost wholly of grey-pink boulder-screes, which are piled up here and there into fantastic buttresses that seem ready to tumble down in the next gust of wind.

Only occasionally has an intrusion of tougher fine-grained granite, the kind of stuff of which tors are made, survived millennia of wind, frost and rain, and still sits in the scree like a huge lump of black iron, rusty with lichen and welded into the mountain with brimstone, truthfully imitated by a yellow lichen which has a way of growing where solid rock and loose scree meet. These black outcrops suggest a railway engine or an old-fashioned kitchen range, and faintly—should your tired fancy run that way—Hell. Possibly the She Devil or the Cailleach have had something to do with this—I would not know.

Be this as it may, the fiacaills between these corries present no
serious difficulty and could be used on the way up or down
Braeriach. The same is largely true of the spur of the Angel's
Peak between An Garbh Choire and Coire an Lochain Uaine.
It looks impressively rocky and has been described as a climb,
but when I took a climbing party there we found nothing to do,
or, to be exact, had to improvise minor climbing pitches on the
sides. The ridge itself is no more than a scramble, though
quite an airy one.

The Angel's Peak and the neighbouring Cairn Toul (4,241
feet) can, of course, be reached without any trouble from the
Great Moss or from Braeriach, with which they form a con-
tinuous twisted whaleback with little variation in altitude
between the summits. The whaleback ends up with the Devil's
Point, an ice-licked rocky promontory (3,303 feet) between
Corrour Bothy and Glen Geusachan. It is quite usual to walk
the whole length of the ridge, but a direct descent from the
Devil's Point, whose lower slopes are precipitous and encased
in boiler-plate slabs with imbricated jointing, is a climbing
proposition. You will have, therefore, to retrace your steps to
the col, some 300 feet below, giving on the Coire Odhar (not to
be confused with the like-named corrie over Loch Einich) of
Cairn Toul and so on to Corrour Bothy at its foot.

The Grey Corrie (Coire Odhar) has a little rock round the
sides, but it nowhere coalesces into cliffs, and the central part,
though steep, is vegetated and presents no difficulty. This is, in
fact, the normal way of tackling Cairn Toul or the traverse of
the Great Moss to Glen Feshie from Corrour Bothy. Cloudberry plants are quite abundant in the corrie, but the berries are
always scarce.

Farther north, Cairn Toul has three more corries: Coire an
t-Saighdeir (at t-Ahjer), the Soldier's Corrie; the little Coire
an t-Sabhail (an t-Owl), Corrie of the Barn, a grassy or sedgy
hollow perched high up, right below the summit; and Coire
an Lochain Uaine, containing the largest and finest of the three
Green Lochans. The first and the third corrie are rocky, but
their ramparts are incomplete, and intervening scree-slopes
afford practicable ways up and down, as do the dividing fiacaills.

Glen Geusachan, whose high portals are the Devil's Point and Beinn Bhrotain (3,795 feet), is a flat-bottomed, rock-bound box of a glen, occupied by a wet meadow, which may be a silted-up loch, and down which the substantial stream, issuing from Loch nan Stuirteag and reinforced by burns foaming down the steep hillsides meanders in a silver ribbon. The glen is a deer sanctuary and the natural gateway from the Central Cairngorms to the Great Moss. Its Gaelic name means Valley of Pines. Nowadays it is completely treeless (see p. 20), but bleached trunks and stumps, embedded in the peaty soil, are scattered all over it to give substance to the name.

Glen Geusachan faces the gap of Allt Preas nam Meirleach, over which a path runs from Glen Luibeg to the Lairig Ghru, and Glen Dee widens here into a diamond, which is over a mile wide. The grey rock bastions of the Devil's Point and Beinn Bhrotain stand up to a thousand feet high. The glaciers came up at Beinn Bhrotain along three intersecting lines and have ground in it three flat faces, which stand out sharp and clear as though fashioned but yesterday. Alternatively hushed or windy, this is a solemn place, and I have christened it " the Hall of the Cairngorms."

Beinn Bhrotain is quite a mountain and well worth a visit. Apart from the Glen Geusachan side, it is devoid of crags and the gradients are moderate. A col, some 600 feet deep, divides it from Monadh Mòr (3,651 feet), and north of the col Coire Cath nam Fionn (Corrie of the Fingalians' Battle), rimmed with scattered rocks, spills into Glen Geusachan, and may be used as an approach to either peak. Southwards the rich stream of Allt Dhàidh Mòr flows from the col into the Geldie Burn over 4 miles or so of rather desolate moor. Glen Geldie is generally a sad glen. The big hills have turned their backs on it and the views are uninspiring. The pot-holed road, ruined buildings and tumble-down bridges complete the picture. It makes a long crossing to Glen Feshie, 8 miles away by road and footpath from the White Bridge on the Dee, and the upper three miles of Glen Feshie continue in the same vein.

CHAPTER TEN

Along and Above the Fairy Stream

THE name Glen Feshie is a corruption of the Gaelic *Gleann Féisidh*, meaning ' Glen of the Fairy Stream,' a beautiful name for possibly the most beautiful and, considering its length, the most uniformly interesting of the Cairngorm glens. Good things often come last, and Glen Feshie is, as we know, the western march of these mountains. In the south, where the river makes an elbow turn, its line is continued by Glen Geldie, already referred to in the preceding chapter.

Between them the two glens make another natural ' mounth ' connecting Speyside with Deeside and duly carry a right-of-way road and path from Kingussie or Kincraig to Braemar. The distance, counted from either of the former, is about 32 miles.

From Kingussie the route runs by road over the Spey Bridge at Ruthven to the Tromie Bridge, a little way beyond which a forest track leads up steeply through a pinewood to the little hamlet of Drumguish, where the line is picked up by a rough road, passable for cycles. This crosses a wide, open moor with scattered pines, rising gently towards a low scarp, below which a small river, sparsely lined with trees, is spanned by a footbridge. The footbridge is somewhat off the main track, which leads to a ford. Both give access to the green flats of Balguish and a lonely shepherd's cottage. Our next landmark is an old sheep-fank across the flats, where we can follow either the clear cart track to lower Glen Feshie, which it reaches half-a-mile below Stronetoper, or a footpath climbing southwards over gentle heather-slopes, to cross the hill about two miles upstream near the head keeper's cottage and a footbridge over the Feshie. The decisive point is how much you carry: heavily-laden people will find the first variant preferable, especially in bad weather.

The Kincraig approach is more interesting. We have here the choice of two routes: one by way of the village of Insh, beyond the wide waters of Loch Insh and some two road-miles from Kincraig, and thence by a metalled road from Balnespick to the pines of Badan Dubh (Black Grove) and over a bridge along a road following the left (west) bank of the Feshie; the other by way of Feshiebridge, crossing the bridge and continuing south, past a ' clachan ' of cottages, to the open moors at the foot of Creag Mhigeachaidh (Vigayhay, 2,429 feet), whose triangular scarp of rock and scree dominates the view. Here, a rough road leads up the east side of Glen Feshie all the way to Achlean. We pass this croft on the river side, cross the swaying footbridge by the Stronetoper school-house and regain the main road. The latter, which is in no great condition, runs up to about a mile beyond Glenfeshie Lodge.

Most of the old forest that used to be the pride of the middle part of the glen was felled during the last war, but a high fringe was left standing, as well as scattered trees and a few solid blocks of pine on both sides of the glen, to keep company to the clear stream, now spreading wide over tinkling stony shallows, now gathering into a deep channel between high banks of glacial drift.

Beyond the lodge the glen widens into green alluvial flats at the foot of the steep blunt hill of Creag na Caillich (2,333 feet), which rises over them like the prow of a ship. Higher up the glen splits into three branches, but both the western ones are blind alleys, and if you follow either of the roads and footpaths from the lodge you will miss upper Glen Feshie. The north-east side of Creag na Caillich is undercut by a scarp and steep screes run straight down to the water's edge. There is no path here.

It is possible to wade the river over the shallows beyond the lodge, but it is much better to take the footbridge at the head keeper's cottage to the east side of the river, where the proper ' mounth ' runs past Landseer's Bothy, which contains a glazed drawing of two stags and a hind executed by the famous artist on the plaster above the fireplace, to the rocky defile between Creag na Caillich and Creag nan Gaibhre (2,411feet).

The scenery associated with goats (*gaibhre*) and the Old Woman or Witch (*Caillich*) is usually rugged. In fact, the latter may be none other than the dreaded *Cailleach Bheur*, a blue giantess with a black face, who used to wander over the hills on a dark stormy night and wail pitifully at the door, craving admittance, but woe to him who would let her in! She was the personification of female malevolence and had her opposite in the kind and beautiful young goddess Bride. However, this is another story.

The rock scarps of the two hills are not very high, but they are raised about 1,000 feet above the floor of the glen, which is rather flat withal, and less than half-a-mile apart. Thus the hillsides are very steep and scarred with rapid screes. Foaming burns hang their threads of frayed white silk over the crags and waterfalls gurgle down rocky troughs. Down below thick-set, cedar-like Caledonian firs dispute possession of the grassy and pebbly levels with alders and birches, while the crystalline water of the Feshie spills over steps and hollows, up which salmon can be seen leaping in the autumn.

This is an enchanted place where peace and strife, Cailleach and Bride, have met and blended in graceful harmony of form, which would have been lost beyond redemption had the long-mooted road to Braemar been built.

Beyond the glacial defile the glen takes on a milder, bucolic look. Green flats, studded with grey boulders, carpet the riverside between the heathery hills, which grow lower and lower, eventually to subside into the mournful bogs of upper Glen Geldie. Meantime small groves and clumps of birch and pine still hug the western slopes, but as the river veers east the scene changes once more. The trees disappear and you will have to walk several miles down the Geldie Burn to see the first few stray birches. Yet at one time Glen Geldie, too, was thickly wooded. The forest used to climb high up the sides of Beinn Bhrotain and Monadh Mòr, where bleached skeletons of pine moulder in the peat.

Half-a-mile beyond the confluence with the Eidart the Feshie turns sharply east and so passes out of Cairngorm country. Less than an eighth of a mile divides the river's bend from the head of the Geldie Burn, but the Braemar path branches off half-a-mile short of it and follows the northern hillsides. There used to be a footbridge over the Eidart, which the river periodically washed away. I do not know whether it still exists or not—the Tourist Map does not show it. In dry weather the Eidart can be crossed without difficulty, but it carries quite a lot of water from the Great Moss, and after a heavy rainstorm or when the snows are melting on the High Tops it is a different story, and a detour upstream may become necessary.

The ' mounth ' as a whole is negotiable by bicycle, and the ' tigers ' who think nothing of taking their mounts over the Lairig Ghru find it ' easy.' You are welcome to try—not me . . .

All this time we have been following the lower edge of the Great Moss. In fact, we could have taken the left fork of the path beside a bothy a quarter of a mile short of the Eidart and after some three miles reached the rocky head of Glen Eidart, where the path peters out and deer tracks take over, leading to the Great Moss above Coire Mharconaich, another three miles on. This is a rather unusual and roundabout approach to the Great Moss, but if you are based on Glen Feshie you may continue up river to Allt Sgairnich and catch there the stalking path, which will take you back over Càrn Bàn Mòr. A crossing to Corrour Bothy can be made by following Allt Luineag on the right and contouring the slopes of Cairn Toul above Loch nan Stuirteag.

Between Coire Mharconaich and middle Glen Feshie rise two dumpy summits, which are little more than upraised edges

of the Great Moss: Diollaid Coire Eindart (3,184 feet) and
Mullach Clach a'Bhlàir (a Vlar, 3,338 feet). There is not much
to say about the first, but the second is of somewhat more
interest inasmuch as it overlooks Glen Feshie and throws out
towards Creag nan Gaibhre an obtuse ridge, called Druim nam
Bò (Cattle Ridge), which is lightly buttressed with crags in the
north, over Coire Domhaim (Down). The ridge ends up at
Lochan nam Bò, perched above Creag nan Gaibhre, towards
which a path zigzags up from Landseer's Bothy.

The Glenfeshie sidings of the Cairngorms pass through three
distinct stages. Above the 3,000-foot contour we have the

Coire Garbhlach

gradual pre-glacial slopes; below it the ground shelves down abruptly to a point, which lies at about 2,000 feet a.s.l. in the upper part of the glen, but climbs steadily down: to 1,500 feet between the head keeper's cottage and Achlean, and to 1,200 feet below the latter. This is the glacial slope, except that in the defile there is a secondary glacial slope from roughly 1,000 to 2,000 feet. The bottom of the glen is flat in accordance with the U-shaped profile of a glacial valley, and between it and the foot of the glacial slopes extend gentle heathery moorlands, largely covered with drift deposits and lightly sculptured by post-glacial streams.

Mullach Clach a'Bhlàir, apart from the upper portion of Coire Domhaim, is gentle on all sides, as its name implies. A path ascends towards the corrie from the footbridge above the head keeper's cottage, and another follows the course of Allt Choire Chaoil (Stream of the Narrow Corrie), farther north, to the edge of Coire Garbhlach.

The latter is remarkable as the only rocky corrie facing due west. It is, however, not the typical cauldron, but a pear-shaped elongated recess, narrowing down into a gorge in its bottom part. As usual the highest cliffs face north, but even these, though scenically impressive, are of no great climbing account. The southward scarp is much broken up, and the rocks at the head of the corrie are discontinuous, affording steep but easy descents over scree and grass from the edge of the Great Moss, best by way of the small secondary corrie—Fionnar Choire (the Cool Corrie) in the north below the summit of Meall Dubhag (3,268 feet).

A green secluded meadow, where deer often graze, spreads at the bottom of the corrie, which is well protected from the chilling winds and where plants often flower long after their usual season. This is one example of the many ' local climates,' typical of mountains in general and of the Cairngorms in particular, where south-easterly slopes usually support the richest vegetation.

The Devil's Point, Glen Geusachan and Beinn Bhrotain, from Càrn a' Mhaim.

Loch Einich and the Sgorans.

The rocks of Coire Garbhlach are schist and gneiss, but granite boulders lie scattered along the bed of the burn, showing that the Cairngorm batholith is nigh.

Meall Dubhag and its neighbour Càrn Bàn Mòr (3,443 feet), enclosing Coire Gorm above Achlean, are individualized even less than Diollaid Coire Eindart and Mullach Clach a'Bhlàir. They dome up gently from a vast plateau, little more than triangulation points. Càrn Bàn Mòr, however, is of some importance because it carries the stalking path from Achlean to the Great Moss and has a little bothy in Ciste Mearearaid (Margaret's 'Kist' which may be a Chest or a Coffin—she has another on Cairn Gorm) below the summit. The 'Kist' is said to be the place where Margaret, a jilted shepherdess, half-insane with sorrow, succumbed to exhaustion after wandering for days over the hills without food or shelter. This is the 'coffin' version. According to the 'chest' story she used to hide here under the snow the cairngorm stones she found. Both versions may be true, but she certainly could not have died on Cairn Gorm as well.

Both Margaret's Chests hold pockets of snow well into the summer, and in the Glen Feshie one a burn bubbles up from a hollow, which is intensely green among the prevailing greyness of the summit upland. Càrn Bàn Mòr is the Great White Cairn, and it does look a little hoary at times, partly because of the grey pebbles with which it is generously strewn, but mainly thanks to a thick growth of golden-moss. This moss can be golden, but its most usual colour is somewhere between ash and dirty soap-suds, which it greatly resembles.

Two big cairns mark the main summit. which is succeeded in the north-west by a further indistinct rotundity. If you continue in this direction Loch Einich will open to your view. There is a kind of path, playing hide-and-seek with scree, grass and heather, and gradually becoming more and more definite as it descends, which leads down to the loch at the foot of the Sgorans and eventually crosses the ancient sluice below the loch to join the Braeriach track at the ruin of John of Corrour's Bothy.

G

The scene is one of dark magnificence. Colonel Thornton, author of *The Sporting Tour*, followed the ridge of the Sgorans from Càrn Bàn Mòr in 1804 with a train of guides and porters, it seems in ' great trepidation,' and put the height of the scarp at no less than 10,000 feet. It has shrunk considerably since his days. The loch lies at 1,650 feet and Sgòr Gaoith, the highest of the Sgorans, stands 3,658 feet above sea level, the next highest Sgòran Dubh Mòr, Great Black Sgoran, is 3 feet lower, so that the drop is about 2,000 feet. Across the loch Braeriach heaves ponderously and steeply, if not ruggedly, to over 4,000 feet. At the head of the loch the 1,000-foot scarp of Coire Odhar is crowned with a frieze of broken cliffs and ice-polished bluffs, over which the waters of Loch nan Cnapan pour down from the Great Moss in several waterfalls. But all this would be nothing without the shadow side of the Sgorans, towering over the inky Loch Einich in ramparts of black granite, oversteepened at the base by the mighty glacier, which has ground the loch's basin 160 feet deep, grey rivers of scree, cones of debris and small grassy corries suspended among them.

A closer inspection will reveal that the rocks are made up of a system of steep ribs or ridges that do not stand high above the bordering scree-shoots, over which it is possible to scramble down to the loch with comparative ease. Down rather than up, because this is the way scree naturally tends to move, and, provided you are properly shod and do not panic at the ground giving way under you, this movement can be utilized for downward escalation, an adaptation that is not possible in reverse.

Still, you will recall that graveyard at Pityoulish. The rocks of the Sgorans are not be to trifled with, and afford some tough climbing routes.

So long, though, as you stay above there are no dangers to contend with, except possibly a storm. Càrn Bàn Mòr spills down very gently towards the Sgorans in a flattish upland about half-a-mile across. The gradient steepens above Coire na Caillich and the Pinnacle Ridge, in which a'Chailleach rears her gaunt 50-foot figure, and the upland narrows down into a crest towards the rocky point of Sgòr Gaoith, whose cairn is perched right on the brink of a substantial precipice. Sgòran Dubh Mòr is a mile farther on. It sends out a side ridge to Geal-chàrn (3,019 feet) and Creag Mhigeachaidh (2,429 feet), overlooking Kincraig and Loch Insh (see pp. 37-38). But the main crest continues northwards to Creag Dubh (2,747 feet) and the terraced height of Cadha Mòr (2,324 feet), 3 and 4 miles on respectively, with minor fluctuations in the generally declining altitude. All this adds up to a pleasant ridge walk, ending over the forests of Inchriach and Rothiemurchus, with Loch an Eilein and Loch Gamhna (pr. Gown) ensconced between wooded hills that hedge them off the Spey. The lochs have road connections on both sides with Kincraig and Aviemore, both of which are 4 miles from Loch an Eilein as the crow flies.

Loch an Eilein, meaning Loch of the Island, is a popular beauty spot, much photographed and painted. Its chief title to fame is a castle built on piles on an islet off the north-western shore. The castle dates from the thirteenth century and once was a stronghold of the mighty Norman family of Comyns, Lords of Badenoch, who had held sway over these lands until they were waylaid by Farquhar Shaw and foully slain on Calart Hill near Pityoulish (p. 68). What happened after this is not quite clear, but somehow or other the Rothiemurchus country passed on to the Shaws, who, however, incurred royal displeasure sometime in the sixteenth century and were in their turn evicted by the Grants. The last occasion on which the castle is mentioned in the annals was in 1715, when a Mackintosh of Balnespick and a few of his adherents were detained there, to prevent their joining the Hanoverians. Today it is a ruin, grown with ivy and flanked with trees. It faces the shore with a blank wall, pierced by a single doorway, which leads straight into the water.

At one time ospreys used to nest on the castle, but they were driven away by the tourists, trying out the echo and putting to the test the statement that the castle " is only a stone's throw from the shore." For a time the harassed birds had found refuge in the trees of Loch Gamhna, but egg collectors soon put a stop to that, and the osprey had disappeared from the Cairngorms for over 120 years until its eventual return to Loch Garten (p. 65).

Loch an Eilein is quite deep, attains 66 feet, and has a number of springs at the bottom which keep it unfrozen even of a hard winter. It was, however, solidly under ice in 1946/47 and I skied right across it. Nevertheless, those who fancy skating on the loch had better first read the inscription on the memorial by the old gean tree near the shore.

History, ospreys, echoes, ski-ing and skating apart, this is pleasant wooded country, with grassy glades sprinkled with primroses in spring and silver birches climbing the sides of the hummocky Ord Ban (1,404 feet) above Loch an Eilein. Beyond Loch Gamhna towards Feshiebridge there is a stretch of fine parkland pinewood, whence a pathway runs up Creag Follais (2,262 feet), an outlier of Creag Dubh.

Those following the ridge down from the Sgorans are well advised to strike this path, which will save them the trouble of descending the awkward heathery slopes of Cadha Mòr farther north. Another way of escape from the Sgoran ridge is by way of Geal-chàrn, which, too, is approached by a forest path from Ballachroick in lower Glen Feshie.

CHAPTER ELEVEN

Eastward Ho!

THE Lairig an Lui from the fords of Avon to the confluence of the Lui Water with the Dee, half-a-mile below the Linn, clearly cuts off the Eastern from the Central Cairngorms. Hence the march runs east with a slight northerly deviation along the Dee as far as Invercauld House (or Castle), taking in Inverey, Mar Lodge and Braemar on the way, to continue to Bealach Dearg and Loch Builg. Glen Quoich and Gleann an t-Slugain (t-Lugan) are the main valleys descending towards Braemar from the heights of Beinn a'Bhùird (3,924 feet) and Ben Avon (3,843 feet), the twin giants of the East. Glen Quoich and its westward tributary valley of Dubh Ghleann shelter some beautiful remnants of the Old Caledonian Forest, and in its lower course the Quoich Water forms interesting falls and gorges, as well as the famous Earl of Mar's Punchbowl, after which the glen is named—*quoich* (caweekh) meaning ' bowl.'

This is a deep pot-hole in which the Earl of Mar mixed a fabulous punch for the success of the rising of 1715. The occasion, however, was marred by an ill-omen when the gold knob fell off the Stuart standard as it was unfurled—perhaps it caught a gust of wind from Sheriffmuir . . .

Gleann an t-Slugain leads straight into the heart of the Eastern Cairngorms. Through it, too, runs the ' mounth ' to Tomintoul—up to the small ruinous lodge at the head of the glen and over a low watershed to Glen Quoich, where the path

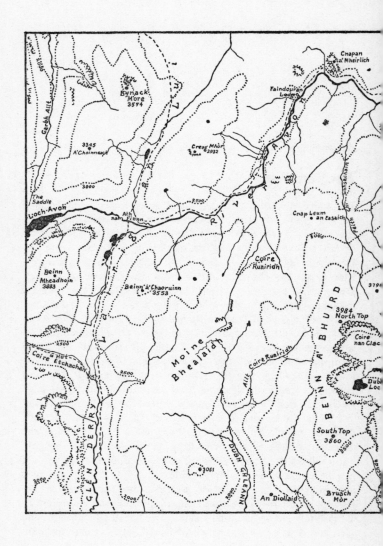

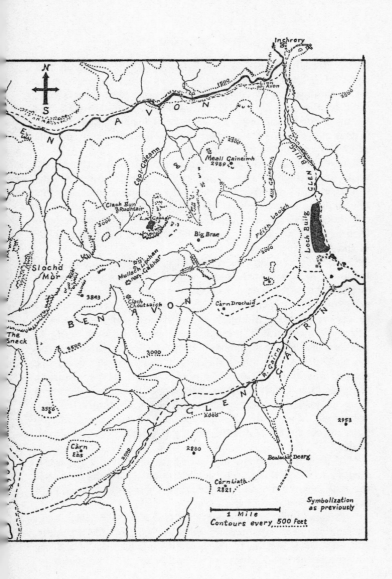

forks. Its left prong leads to Beinn a'Bhùird and is on this occasion no business of ours. We follow the right prong as far as the heathery base of Càrn Eas Beag. Here a clear pass indicates the head of Glen Gairn. This is our present goal, and we must not let the apparent absence of a path disconcert us; it does materialize a little higher up, and it would be pure waste of time trying to find it too soon.

There is nothing of great interest in Glen Gairn, though we could use it to climb Ben Avon if we felt tired of other routes; it is as plain as any glen can be until we come to the sad ruins of a shooting lodge (5 miles) above Loch Builg. The 'mounth' continues along the east bank of the loch, down Glen Builg to Inchrory and thence to Tomintoul through the green valley of the Avon.

Glen Builg can also be reached by road from Balmoral or Ballater, and it was at the latter that one day of mixed sunshine and cloud I hired a taxi to convey me to Corndavon Lodge, three miles short of the loch. The driver swore it was impossible to get any farther, although in my modest opinion the road below the lodge was in a much worse condition than above it. Be this as it may, the aged but still powerful Rolls-Royce whisked me up and down the steep inclines of narrow roads as my eye roamed idly about. The views were not particularly inspiring, as upper Glen Gairn is treeless and monotonous, with here and there a lonely cottage and an occasional glimpse of the 'pimpled' Ben Avon. At half past one I was again on my light and ready feet beside the small grove sheltering Corndavon Lodge.

Half an hour later saw me among the cluster of tarns introductory to Loch Builg. The sun came out scorching as I shut the gate behind me and stepped upon the right-of-way path skirting the east side of the loch.

Although in itself a fine sheet of water, Loch Builg is lacking in distinction. The surrounding hillsides are low and formless, and only the flowering of the heather and the play of the sky can redeem the insignificance of its prospects. I did not pause to

Lochan nan Gabhar.

The wind-scoured heights of Ben Avon from Beinn a' Bhuird.

Glen Quoich.

A perfect summer's day in the heart of the Cairngorms. On the summit of Braeriach looking towards Cairn Toul and the Angel's Peak.

admire these, but at the other end yielded to the warmth of the sun and the glitter of ripples to subside into the heather in a lazy reverie. Now the dark would gain most of the offshore mirror, now the bright silver bring the whole loch under its sway, driving the murky tremors into the shelter of little bays and boulders. There was rest in water, mother of all life, and I closed my eyes against the bright sunshine in the scarlet glare of blood. The tinkle of wavelets entered my ears, and my awareness sank into the subconscious world of scattered images. Unwillingly, I roused myself from my stupor and slipped my arms under the straps of my rucksack.

In a few minutes my feet struck the clanking limestone scree, and a sudden abundance of flowers marked the richer soil. Milkworts, daisies, thyme, clover and multitudes of nodding yellow rock-roses were scattered broadcast along the path winding down into Glen Builg. The sterile granite had retreated up the western hillsides, grown solid with ling, which had given way in the east to pale limestone grass. Outcrops of pigeon-blue and ash-grey rock had replaced the pink and black boulders. Some junipers and birches, spared by the heather conflagrations, were still lining the gullies of the burns where the fires had been checked, and farther down the glen singed trees were struggling to revive among the charred branchless trunks of their less lucky companions. Higher up the eastern slopes red scree and soil disclosed the presence of the overlying red sandstone, which became more prominent towards Tomintoul.

In a green depression I tasted of the soft limestone water, and mounted the path that cut across a steep grassy slope winking in the breeze with innumerable rock-roses, which seemed to grow here to an exceptional size. The white-washed Inchrory Lodge was now in sight behind a pleasant birch grove. Meanwhile the clouds had gathered over the hills into a lowering canopy, which presently released a sharp shower.

At Inchrory the Avon forms a 'crossroads.' Having issued from Loch Avon, twelve miles to the west, it follows an easterly course, but swings sharply north towards Tomintoul, upon taking in the Builg Burn. At one time, however, it used to continue eastwards and fall into the Don, and the low pass which faces Glen Avon above the lodge is part of its erstwhile bed. It stands only about a hundred feet above the present bed, and a cart track crosses it to Dalnadamph Lodge.

The change appears to have been due to the erosion by a glacier sliding down Glen Builg.

The lower reaches of Glen Avon are rather monotonous and drab. You can have a peep on the way into the wide rocky cauldron of Muckle Slock (Slochd Mòr) and Sma Glen, but there are not many points where this can be done, and the average pictorial interest of Glen Avon is low. Cnapan a'Mheirlich, the Reivers' Knoll, a little rocky hill (2,252 feet), partnering a smaller Cnap an Dobhrain (the Otter's Knoll, 2,276 feet), mark the approaches to Faindouran Lodge, seven miles up the glen from Inchrory and 4½ miles short of Loch Avon. The lodge, standing at 1,920 feet above sea-level, is claimed to be the highest in Scotland and is still habitable, though normally unoccupied. Its ' bothy end ' is open for the use of climbers and walkers, which is very welcome in this distant and devious part of the hills.

It is well placed for exploring Beinn a'Bhùird, which can be climbed easily from this side by way of Coire Ruairidh or Cnap Leum an Easaich, Slochd Mòr and Ben Avon, accessible by any of the shoulders dipping into Glen Avon and, more distantly, the surroundings of Loch Avon.

The part of the Eastern Cairngorms between Faindouran Lodge and Glen Derry is undistinguished. It is occupied by high moors, somewhat reminiscent of the Great Moss, but rather lower and less compact. This is Moine Bhealaidh (Moin Velakh), known more popularly in English as the Broom or Yellow Moss, a favourite haunt of deer herds, some 2,800 feet high on the average and bounded north and south by Beinn a'Chaorruinn (3,553 feet), which rises over the Moss in a regular cone, and Beinn Bhreac (3,051 feet), thrust between Dubh Ghleann and Glen Derry. The latter makes a good viewpoint for

Derry Cairngorm, backed up by Ben Macdhui, and dips steeply over 1,000 feet towards the parkland forest of Dubh Ghleann.

The line is continued south-eastwards by two more dumpy hills: Meall an Lundain (2,560 feet) and Creag Bhalg (2,190 feet), which may look fine when heather is in bloom but have little to offer to a summer visitor. Between them the narrow pass of Clais Fhearnaig makes a useful crossing from Glen Lui to Glen Quoich and carries a path which joins Duke of Fife's old cart track from Mar Lodge, continued by a path to An Diollaid, an outlier of Beinn a'Bhùird. This is, indeed, one of the most popular ways of climbing the great ben, with Dubh Ghleann as a possible variant.

Creag Bhalg, stooping over Mar Lodge, carries two ski-tows and in winter is a hive of activity, but is of no special interest in summer. It makes an inferior viewpoint. The Eastern Cairngorms are singularly inward, retiring mountains, which reserve their grandest scenery for those who venture into their midst. From the distance one can at best glean a glimpse of a rock scarp over one or another of their corries from a turn of some road or path, but never more than that. Creag Bhalg offers no great improvement on this, but its higher neighbour across Glen Quoich, Càrn na Drochaide (2,681 feet) does. It looks right up Glen Quoich towards the great eastern corries of Beinn a'Bhùird, though the northern cliffs of Garbh Choire and the corries of Ben Avon remain hidden from sight.

Beinn a'Bhùird is the Table Mountain with a characteristically flat top, carved out of the dismembered High Tableland. The marks of dismemberment are the encroaching glens and corries. The configuration of the mountain is determined by the fork of Glen Quoich and Dubh Ghleann, which embrace it from the south, while in the north the broad scoop of Muckle Slock enters deep into the mountain mass. From the Broom Moss in the west Beinn a'Bhùird swells up in a thousand-foot billow. This is moderately steep half-way up, but nearly level at the top, where it forms the characteristic 'Table' that gives the mountain its name. Even so there is really less flat ground here than on Braeriach or Ben Macdhui, although an aircraft successfully crash-landed on Beinn a'Bhùird during the late war. The 'Table' is two-miles-long and culminates in two indistinct prominences near its opposite ends, known as the North and the South Top respectively. The first is the higher of the two (3,924 feet), but the difference does not exceed 60 feet, while the lowest point of the 'Table' lies only 100 feet below it. Here, in a green hollow where snow often lies in the summer, is the source of the copious burn, flowing south, parallel to the summit crest. It is this Alltan na Beinne that has separated off a fold of the ground called An Diollaid, which carries a path already referred to on page 95.

Another stream (Allt Coire Ruaridh) rises below the North Top and flows in to the Black Glen (Dubh Ghleann). The North Top is a surveyor's affair and would pass unnoticed save for the cairn that marks it. The upper part of Glen Quoich is shaped like a five-lobed leaf, the three eastern lobes composing the rocky corries of Beinn a'Bhùird: Coire na Ciche (Corrie of the Breast); Coire an Dubh Lochain, containing a handsome moraine tarn at the foot of the cliffs and a further ragged strip of water on a lower step of the corrie; and the boulder-strewn Coire nan Clach (Corrie of Stones). The central lobe leads to the Sneck, a low col (about 3,200 feet) overlooking the two-mile Muckle Slock and dividing Beinn a'Bhùird from Ben Avon in the east. The fifth lobe is a shallow rockless corrie between two outliers of Ben Avon known jointly as Càrn Eas, Mòr and Beag (3,556 feet and 3,189 feet respectively).

At its north end the 'Table' turns eastwards and expands into an undulating upland about a mile long towards the Sneck and half as wide south to north, where it throws out a ridge towards Stob an t-Sluichd (3,621 feet). This ridge carries the stalking path from Glen Avon and frames the rocky recess of Garbh Choire, a close rival of its namesake in Braeriach and, indeed, superior to it from the climber's point of view.

Below the Sneck, however, which is overlooked by Cnap a'Chléirich, the Clergyman's Knoll (3,811 feet), sometimes referred to as the Third Eastern Cairngorm, the rock fringe is fragmentary and a practicable deer track winds through it to the pass. The same is largely true of the Ben Avon side, which though steep has nothing to compare with the formidable buttresses of Garbh Choire. Nevertheless, Leabaidh an Daimh Buidhe (Couch of the Yellow Stag), the summit tor of Ben Avon, stands about 1,600 feet over the floor of Slochd Mòr and the total scenic effect is considerable.

Cnap a'Chléirich is accessible on all sides save that of Garbh Choire, and Coire nan Clach can be negotiated without climbing at several points, although some mossy slabs may prove troublesome when wet. The corrie is divided from Coire an Dubh Lochain by a steep rocky fiacaill, and the latter corrie terminates southwards in an 800 foot black granite buttress of A'Chioch (The Breast), a prominent local landmark, beyond which the rock frieze largely disintegrates into steep scree.

The ground about the South Top of Beinn a'Bhùird is not nearly so flat as farther north. Its gritty wind terraces are enlivened in midsummer with a fine growth of sea thrift and moss campion, and the peak falls away steeply over 2,000 feet and more towards the central portion of Glen Quoich, which continues the line of Glen Gairn. This is a beautiful but trackless stretch of country, ancient pines lining the water and ascending in places almost to the 2,000-foot contour. The glen used to be thickly wooded, but most of the trees were uprooted in the great storm of 1893 and their mouldering trunks lie where they fell. High up the hill some veteran firs have died of old age, as it were, in their boots and their barkless and leafless skeletons still gleam, weirdly erect, over the long, unburned heather.

In the east, where the Quoich Water points north, the Slugan path (p. 92) forks, and its one prong ascends Càrn Fiàclach towards the South Top and so marks a route to Beinn a'Bhùird, which makes a long steady pull. The other prong continues to the ruined bothy of Clach a'Chléirich (Clergyman's Rock) and so to Coire nan Clach and the Sneck (3 miles).

Above the latter Ben Avon rises steeply at first for about 300 feet, to spread into a plateau above the 3,500-foot contour, paralleling the upland between Cnap a'Chléirich and the North Top of Beinn a'Bhùird; but towards the Couch of the Yellow Stag it narrows into a ridge. The latter curves round the corrie of Allt an Eàs Mhòr into a kind of horseshoe, studded with tors and ending up in the east in Stuc Gharbh Mhòr above Glen Gairn. The slopes here have the usual glacial configuration, gentle up to 2,500 feet, then steep to 3,250 and gradually easing off into the flat summit upland. None of them present any difficulty except that of approach, as this side of the mountain is miles from nowhere.

Strictly speaking, Ben Avon is not a single mountain but a whole range with a number of clearly marked subsidiary summits. Nearly all of these carry excrescences of dark granite of varying height, and other tors are scattered over the plateaux, shoulders and spurs of the massif, giving it a distinctive appearance. This is rather bewildering in the mist, as it is difficult to tell at a glance which tor is which. The south-eastern hillsides are grass- and heather-grown; the western sidings are barren and gravelly.

Eastwards, above Loch Builg, the Glen of Féith Laoigh (the Calf Burn) splits the massif into two chains of minor heights. Of these the Big Brae, rising into a sugarloaf of 3,354 feet, dominates the Builg views. Yet the loch itself lies at 1,568 feet above sea-level, so that the general effect is subdued, all the higher summits being hidden from sight.

The most interesting part of Ben Avon is in the north, along Glen Avon. The Muckle Slock is there, as well as the Little Slock, or Slochd Beag, a small rocky corrie between two shoulders of Ben Avon, the higher eastern of which bears the name of Stob Bac an Fhurain (3,533 feet). Its lower slopes are adorned in the east by the remarkable tors of Clach Bun Rudhtair, which look at first sight like the ruins of a castle and attain 80 feet from base to top on the glen side.

Farther east, a dark-green moraine tarn, Lochan nan Gabhar (the Goats' Lochan), fills a concavity of another rocky corrie, and Big Brae sends into Glen Avon two spurs, known as the East and the West Green Finger, and crowned with combs of dumpy rocks, ranging from large boulders to sizeable crags. Meall Gaineimh (Ganay, 2,989 feet), the last outpost of Ben Avon above Inchrory, forms a starting point for the traverse of the massif from this side and carries a partial walking path.

The hill takes its fame from Clach Bhan (Women's Stone), a spacious tor with several round potholes, worn out in the rock by pools of gritty water rotated in the wind. The 'chairing' in one of these was supposed to ensure easy child labour, seemingly because the 'Very Fair One,' the Lady of Fingal, who was swept to her death by the water of A'an at Ath nam Fionn (p. 12), used to bathe in these potholes. In the bygone days Clach Bhan drew a regular pilgrimage of expectant mothers —and it appears that the charm worked.

CHAPTER TWELVE

Across the Eastern Cairngorms

THERE are recurrent weather patterns. On this particular occasion a hot sunny day was invariably followed by a dull one, with often a thunderstorm interposed between them.

The best part of July 25th fell into the first category, only a few clouds wandering like lost sheep about the horizon, although apparently it rained at Nairn. Tomintoul had no rain that day, and its high, windswept moors were dry to walk on. Sitting by the fence on Tom na Bat, a small hill south of the village, I watched the tor-studded outline of Ben Avon, 10-12 miles away, and played with the notion of a scorching day on the High Tops. Yet the next day broke grey, though with promise in the sky, as I was leaving for Inchrory at 7.50 S.T. sharp. It was the early hour of loud footfalls on the flags, before the morning has shaken off the dew from its eyelashes and when the last cobwebs of mist linger on the meadows.

The glen of the Avon was richly green and somnolent below the dull magenta of the hillsides under massed bell-heather in bloom. Kine were lowing as they paced towards their pastures. Grey mists were trailing over the northern hilltops.

I hurried on to ' Birchfield,' three miles up river, where John Wilson, the Inchrory head keeper, had promised me a lift to the Lodge at 9.30. This was going to shorten my itinerary by six miles of road-walking, and I had a long trek to the Derry ahead of me, as well as a heavy rucksack on my back.

I arrived punctually, and, having put our heads together, we decided that Caol Ghleann, or Sma Glen as it is called locally, and the West Green Finger would be the most economic approach to the High Tops, taking in Lochan nan Gabhar, on which I had photographic designs. I said goodbye to John Wilson at 9.15 at Inchrory, crossed the footbridge over the Builg Burn and proceeded up the Avon along the rock trough of the Linn of Avon, enclosed in a spinney of birch and pine, to the uneventful heathlands of its upper glen. The tors stood dark on the foreshortened hillsides and the mist-line was still low. I did not hurry, giving the clouds time to lift and, I hoped, disperse before I had reached Lochan nan Gabhar.

Having negotiated some wet ground at the foot of Sma Glen, I caught a deer track above the burn. Thousands of deer must have passed this way, for the track was wide and so well trodden as to give the impression of an artificial footpath. On my left was a steep rise; uphead the glen opened out into a wide hollow and divided into three branches. The easternmost of these was bounded by the rocky crest of the East Green Finger. The West Green Finger was straight ahead of me, its rocks telescoped into a knob. Above it Big Brae stood out in a massive sugarloaf against the lightening clouds, through which some sunshine was seeping uncertainly. The view gave no indication of the corrie cradling Lochan nan Gabhar, which lay just a little west of and behind the West Green Finger, anything but green from this side. The top of Ben Avon was lost in shifting mists, from which Clach Bun Rudhtair rose in dim outline.

Two roe-deer appeared; first a doe leaping along the ravine of the burn; then a buck crossing the track some twenty yards away in long easy sweeps, like a well-trained racehorse on the turf. Neither took any notice of my camouflaged self. As soon, however, as I removed my off-white anorak, disclosing a sky-blue shirt and a salmon-pink jersey underneath, the buck grew agitated and slowly retreated up the hill with an angry bark. He was obviously in rut, which with roe-deer sets in about a month earlier than with red deer, and very excitable. Half-an-

H

hour later, from a good mile up the glen I could still hear him barking huskily on a commanding knoll on the left skyline.

Walking now on the one, now on the other side of the burn, both of which were rather wet, I found myself at twenty past noon in the elbow of the glen at the foot of the West Green Finger. The hill began steeply but comfortably with a stretch of burned heather followed by a lace of gritty channels, dredged by the spring melt-waters and affecting a kind of zig-zagging pathway.

On the way up I flushed a few grouse and a blue hare. Another roe-deer barked somewhere among the tors. Multitudes of grey geometer moths fluttered up at my every step, their wings imitating the patterns of weathered granite so perfectly as to make them quite invisible on the stones where they alighted.

It was sultry, which made climbing with a heavy pack tiring, and I was glad to take it off and sit down for a long rest in a passage between the rocks overlooking Lochan nan Gabhar. A juvenile wheatear, big and fluffy in the way of young birds, watched me impassively from a few yards away as I unpacked my lunch and camera and made myself comfortable on a patch of soft turf among the boulders. The rocks and the sky in its indeterminate greyness breathed chill. The mists had risen somewhat and the towers of Bun Rudhtair were now clear, though the tops above them remained shrouded in sluggish cloud. A herd of deer was outlined on the green skyline where Big Brae and the wide upland of Mullach Lochan nan Gabhar met in a shallow pass.

The Goats' Lochan sits in a deep, secluded hollow, enclosed by steep and even precipitous grass slopes and in the south by an abrupt hill-face, built up with three tiers of cliff-friezes, none of them particularly high or difficult, but the whole making an impressive setting. Between the crags crescents of grey snow were defying the hot summer and rills hung down in silky threads to the waters of the tarn, pine-green under the frowning sky.

I enjoyed a few scrambles on the tors of the ' coxcomb,' which abounded in short chimneys and somewhat holdless slabs, and, at half-past one, my hopes for better lighting having proved vain, gathered my belongings, crossed to the east side of the ridge and made for the summit cone of Big Brae. This, however, I did not feel like climbing and cut, instead, across the steep incline towards the shallow pass with the deer. The angle increased as I drew nearer to the lochan, which showed finely at my feet between outcrops of dark granite, heaving up from scree-shoots and grassy hillsides. In places the grass was uncomfortably steep, giving scant purchase to the foot, and a rucksack was a little awkward to balance. Dangerous this was not, but after a heavy rain a slip on such ground could be nasty. Anyway, I was pleased to strike a comfortable deer track, which did not require so much attention.

Up above, deer were wallowing in juicy peat-hags among a broad concavity. The view was reminiscent of the Great Moss, but, unlike it, the rise of the Mullach in the south-west was over-spread with a thick, soft and springy carpet of crowberry, azalea, dwarfish bilberry, ochre-tipped sedge and false reindeer moss, which completely hushed my footfalls. I was now walking into the mists, where some tors loomed up like phantom castles of the heights.

For half-an-hour or so I steered south-west by compass, though the mist was never thick enough to make orientation really difficult. Then the cloud lifted, disclosing Coutts' Stone (Clach Choutsaich) on my left, the tors of Stob Bac an Fhurain on my right and the Couch of the Yellow Stag about a mile ahead. Beinn a'Bhùird remained immersed, but there seemed to be sunshine in the Braemar glens, which were suffused with a milky-blue radiance, and the distant Ben y Ghloe showed clear. On the gentle green slopes beneath the bearded fringe of cloud some deer clustered round the snow 'wraith' where Allt an Eàs Mhòr has its source.

I peeped down into Slochd Mòr, but it was like a boiling cauldron from which shaggy mists came spiralling up and spread over the Sneck.

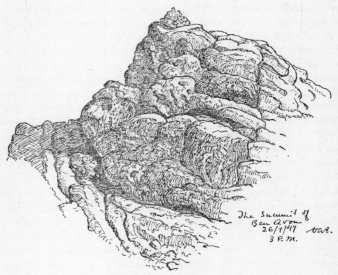

The summit of
Ben Avon
26/7/47 vas.
3 P.M.

The Summit of Ben Avon

Without undue hurry I reached the summit tors of Ben Avon at 2 p.m. S.T. (1 p.m. G.M.T.), just as the cloud curtain went up from the North Top of Beinn a'Bhùird. I was greeted there by a strangely human call, but when I looked round the rocks all I could see was a covey of ptarmigan taking wing.

The summit cairn is perched at the top of the largest tor, which can be climbed along the ridge without much difficulty, though surely no stag of whatever colour could ever have 'couched' there. The granite is weathered into holdless rotundities, assuming shapes reminiscent of Aztec or Maya sculptures, not malevolent like some sharper rocks, but rather portentously childish. There is among them quite a good face—of some stylized Central American Blimp—half-way below the cairn on the east side.

The weather, albeit not unpleasant for hill-walking, was of the heavy unnerving kind. I tried some scree-running down the steep barren slopes in which Ben Avon falls away to the Sneck, but unconvincingly, and it took me about half-an-hour to get there.

A little sun filtered out of the hesitant sky, fingering the rock outcrops, the scree and the green grass-shelf that ran oddly parallel to and a few yards below the line of the pass on the Slochd side, and filling the Rough Corrie of Beinn a'Bhùird with the gloom of shadow, over which clouds piled up, lurid-blue.

Leaden weariness stole upon me as slowly I made my way up the sharp rise of Cnap a'Chléirich.

The wind had left on the grit curious ripple marks, spaced with mathematical precision, as though a harrow had passed over it.

At the top of the Knoll I felt I could walk no farther without a good rest and a drink of water. Fortunately, two burns rise at the edges of the upland, one flowing into Coire nan Clach, the other into Garbh Choire. I chose the latter. The pink jewels of moss campion were still there to greet me—late in the year— and the mossy banks were dry. I filled my mug and lay down on my back, sipping water and chewing chocolate. As usual, the great stillness around me seemed full of strange noises, light footfalls and whispers. The gold wrapping of Cadbury's ' Mild Dessert ' was a gaudy intrusion into the chaste colour scheme of rock, moss and sedge. The clouds gathered into a dense roof and the corries turned to sinister ink. Ben Avon vanished beyond a curtain of mist, and cool moisture suffused the air. Yet it did not rain.

The long rest, the chocolate and the water had refreshed me, and when, at 4 p.m., I resumed my climb my legs carried me swiftly up the gentle grey incline to the cairn of the North Top, to which on a childish impulse I added three small stones. I did not linger there. The sky looked threatening, and I was anxious to slip away from under the descending mists. So I strode down briskly towards the Broom Moss, spreading alarm among the deer herds.

The Moss lay at my feet—a humble, moth-eaten rug of dusty green, pale sienna and peaty-black. Beyond and above, the Central and Western Cairngorms rose in a majestic crowd of peaks, cliffs and corries, among which clouds swelled and subsided, broke up and re-gathered in slow ceaseless unrest, now and then the hidden sun casting sudden gold on a summit or brae.

Breathing the great freedom of the moors, I walked into the western light, which grew redder and redder as I approached the Derry Woods.

I reached Luibeg at 7.45. Not so much my legs as my arms were tired, and strange loquacity came over me.

v.a.z.   Cantharellus cibarius

I *Some distances and walking times*

The approximate distances and/or walking times for the most important crossings and ascents are tabulated below for the reader's convenience. An asterisk (*) marks those times which will apply also if the indicated direction is reversed. When a walk involving both mountain and glen is taken in descent the time will be about $\frac{2}{3}$ of the indicated figure and about $\frac{1}{2}$ if there is little or no glen walking. Distances and differences of level can be obtained from the maps and, unless special difficulties are involved, the fairly accurate rule is to count an hour's walking for every 3 miles plus half-an-hour for each ascent of 1,000 feet.

Most of the data are given after the *Scottish Mountaineering Club Guide*, 3rd Edition (1950). The particulars from the plaque on the Cairngorm Club Bridge over Allt na Beinne in Rothiemurchus are listed first.

From	To	By	Distance miles	Time hours
C.C. Bridge	Aviemore		4	$1\frac{1}{2}$*
,,	Coylumbridge		2	$\frac{3}{4}$*
,,	Lairig Ghru (summit)		$5\frac{1}{2}$	3*
,,	Derry Lodge	L. Ghru and Luibeg	14	$6\frac{1}{2}$*
,,	Linn of Dee	L. Ghru	18	8*
,,	Braemar	L. Ghru	$24\frac{1}{2}$	10*
Derry Lodge	Allt Clach nan Taillear	Gl. Luibeg		$2\frac{1}{2}$*
Braemar	Nethybridge	Lairig an Lui	30	12–13*
Braemar	Derry Lodge		10	$4\frac{1}{2}$
Derry Lodge	Ben Macdhui	Coire Etchachan	$7\frac{1}{2}$	$3\frac{1}{2}$–$4\frac{1}{2}$
Derry Lodge	Ben Macdhui	Gl. Luibeg	$5\frac{1}{2}$	$2\frac{1}{2}$–3
Derry Lodge	Pools of Dee	Gl. Luibeg	$9\frac{1}{2}$	4–$4\frac{1}{2}$
Aviemore	Ben Macdhui	Pools of Dee		7–8
Shelter Stone	Ben Macdhui			$1\frac{1}{2}$–2
Glenmore	Cairn Gorm	Aonaich Shoulder	$4\frac{1}{2}$	$2\frac{1}{2}$–3
Aviemore	Cairn Gorm	Lurcher's Crag	12	5–$6\frac{1}{2}$
Cairn Gorm	Ben Macdhui		4	$1\frac{3}{4}$–2*
Derry Lodge	Cairn Toul	Coire Odhar	7	4–5
Cairn Toul	Braeriach		$3\frac{1}{2}$	$1\frac{1}{2}$–2*
Aviemore	Loch Einich		9	4
Loch Einich (Lower Bothy)	Braeriach (West Top)		3	$2\frac{1}{2}$

From	To	By	Distance miles	Time hours
Loch Einich (Upper Bothy)	Braeriach	Coire Dhondail	4	3–3½
Braemar	Ben Avon	Gl. an t'Slugain	9	4½–5
Inchrory	Ben Avon		6	3½
Inchrory	Loch Avon		12	5
Inchrory	Derry Lodge	B. a'Chaorruinn and Beinn Bhreac		9
Braemar	Beinn a'Bhùird (South Top)	Gl. an t'Slugain	7½	4

II *Bibliography*

An interesting and extensive bibliography of the subject, including many early rare publications, will be found in Sir Henry Alexander's *The Cairngorms* (the official S.M.C. Guide). A selection of the more accessible works with an immediate bearing on hill-walking in the Cairngorms is listed below.

Author	Title	Publisher	Date
ALEXANDER, SIR HENRY	The Cairngorms, 3rd Edition	S.M.C., Edinburgh	1950
BREMNER, ALEXANDER	Physical Geology of the Dee Valley		1912
BURTON, J. HILL	Cairngorm Mountains		1864
CAIRNGORM CLUB	Journal	Cairngorm Club, Aberdeen	
DARLING, FRASER	Natural History in the Highlands and Islands	Collins, London	1947
FIRSOFF, V. A.	The Cairngorms on Foot and Ski	Hale, London	1949
,, ,,	On Ski in the Cairngorms	Chambers, Edinburgh and London	1965
FORSYTH, Rev. W.	In the Shadow of Cairngorm		1900
GORDON, SETON	The Cairngorm Hills of Scotland	Cassell, London	1925
,, ,,	Highways and By-ways in the Central Highlands	Macmillan, London	1948
GRANT, ELIZABETH	Memoirs of a Highland Lady	Murray, London	1928
GRANT, ISABEL FRANCES	Everyday Life on an Old Highland Farm		1924
HUNTER, J. KERR and GULBRANDSEN, ODD	Ski-ing in Britain	Nelson, Edinburgh and London	1963
LOADER, CATHERINE	Cairngorm Adventure at Glenmore Lodge	Brown, Edinburgh	1952
MACBAIN, A.	Place Names of Inverness-shire		1899
McCONNOCHIE, A. I.	Deeside		1895

Author	Title	Publisher	Date
McCROW, BRENDA	Speyside to Deeside	*Oliver & Boyd, Edinburgh*	1956
MEARNS, S. N.	Around Strathspey	*Mearns, Aberdeen*	1948
PERRY, RICHARD	In the High Grampians	*Drummond, London*	1948
,, ,,	The Watcher and the Red Deer	*Hodge, London and Edinburgh*	1952
PLUMB, CHARLES	Walking in the Grampians	*Maclehose, London*	1935
POUCHER, W. A.	A Camera in the Cairngorms	*Chapman & Hall, London*	1947
READ, H. H. and MACGREGOR, A. G.	British Regional Geology: The Grampian Highlands, 2nd Edition	*H.M.S.O., Edinburgh*	1948
SCOTTISH MOUNTAINEERING CLUB	Journal	*S.M.C., Edinburgh*	
WALTON, JOHN (Ed.)	Glen More (National Forest Park Guide)	*H.M.S.O., Edinburgh*	1949